HIDDEN HISTORY
of
LaGRANGE, KENTUCKY

Nancy Stearns Theiss

Published by The History Press
Charleston, SC
www.historypress.com

Copyright © 2022 by Nancy Stearns Theiss
All rights reserved

First published 2022

Manufactured in the United States

ISBN 9781467152341

Library of Congress Control Number: 2022943517

Notice: The information in this book is true and complete to the best of our knowledge. It is offered without guarantee on the part of the author or The History Press. The author and The History Press disclaim all liability in connection with the use of this book.

All rights reserved. No part of this book may be reproduced or transmitted in any form whatsoever without prior written permission from the publisher except in the case of brief quotations embodied in critical articles and reviews.

Contents

Acknowledgements	5
Introduction	7

Part I. How LaGrange Got Its Name
The Marquis de Lafayette	9
The William Berry Taylor Family and Their Influence in the Region	11
The Taylor Families	12
Carlos McDowell, First Mayor, Dies in Tragic Fire	15
Fires in LaGrange	16

Part II. LaGrange and the Train
History and Recollections	18
The Interurban Railroad	25

Part III. The Schools
LaGrange Grade and High School: Origins from Funk Seminary Masonic College	29
The LaGrange Training School: A Rosenwald School	39

Part IV. The Oldham County Courthouse
The Beginning	47
The Civil War	50
Fire Destroyed the Old Courthouse in 1873, Replaced by New Structure in 1875	51

Part V. Special Places
Hendron's Grocery Store	59
The Taylor Addition: West Jefferson Street	61
The McCarty and Ricketts Funeral Home	64
The Frozen Food Locker	66

Contents

Mallory Taylor Hospital — 68
The Belle of LaGrange — 71
Anita Springs and the Royal Inn — 73
The Public Spring — 74

Part VI. Special Homes
William Todd Barbour House — 75
Rob Morris House — 77
Buddy Pepper House — 80
Dr. Hubert Blaydes House and Hospital — 82
David Wark Griffith House — 84
Risley-Head House — 88
James and Amanda Mount House — 90

Part VII. Churches
DeHaven Baptist Church — 93
First Baptist Church of LaGrange — 95
LaGrange Presbyterian Church — 97
LaGrange Methodist Church — 99
LaGrange Kynett Methodist Episcopal Church — 101
LaGrange Christian Church — 104
The Immaculate Conception Church — 109

Part VIII. Main Street LaGrange
Main Street Recollections — 110
Jimmy Oldson's Barber Shop — 116
The LaGrange Post Offices — 118
Ballard Brothers Store — 120
Masonic Lodge, Fortitude Lodge No. 47 — 122
J.R. Gatewood's Drugstore — 123
D.W. Griffith Theatre — 124
The Central Hotel — 125
Kroger — 129
Glauber's Five and Ten Cent Store — 130
McDowell Pharmacy and Head's Drugstore — 132
T.W. Duncan Hardware Store — 136
The Bank of Oldham County — 138
The Saurer Building and Kincaid Hardware Store — 140

Bibliography — 141
About the Author — 144

Acknowledgements

This is my third book that I have written for The History Press, and I am grateful for this publishing company that is dedicated to preserving the stories and history on a local level. As the executive director of the Oldham County History Center since 2004, I get to explore the hidden history of my community every day, and with each day, I learn something more about myself, the place where I grew up and the importance of community. I am thrilled to be able to share my views and experiences in the books that I write. Thanks to Chad Rhoad, my commissioning editor at The History Press, for supporting this manuscript.

Thank you to my board of directors at the Oldham County History Center who enable me to do my job. They understand how local history can direct, change and challenge the community. The support from the board and our faithful members at the Oldham County History Center affirms the importance of preserving our community memory that gives our county a strong sense of historical identity and character.

I am grateful for the support of Peyton Samuel Head Trust and the Mahan Foundation; both have been valued champions of our efforts at the Oldham County History Center, which funds our ongoing research and oral histories. A special recognition to our Oldham County History Center Gala Committee volunteers, who help raise funds that manage our archives and educational programs.

Always a big hug to Judy Fisher, who, as a history center supporter, came into my office one day in 2006 and said, "I just back from New Mexico, and

Acknowledgements

they have this great program, the Santa Fe Living Treasures, that I thought you would like to read about." In 2007, we launched our own Living Treasures Oral History Program thanks to Judy's interest.

A special thanks to my best friend and partner for life, Jim Theiss, who edits, rereads and supports my efforts in writing and always encourages me to go beyond the norm.

Introduction

This book is about the "hidden history" of my hometown of LaGrange, Kentucky. I have included my own research into the town's hidden past with excerpts from interviews of oral histories I have conducted from our Living Treasures Program at the Oldham County History Center.

We created the Living Treasures Program in 2007 to identify people in our local community who are outstanding in their deeds, actions and mentorship during their lifetime. After I interview, transcribe and edit the oral histories, they are sent to our local newspaper, the *Oldham Era*, and published. Professional photographers Peter Campbell and Bobbi Nelson provide a portrait of the Living Treasure who accompanies the published article. We publish the histories once a month, so as of the date of this book's publication, I have conducted 172 Living Treasures oral histories.

Often when interviewing someone, I thought, "Oh, so that is the way it happened," or "Really, sure, I thought so myself." The people I have included in this book grew up in LaGrange when the population was around 2,400. LaGrange was a small town surrounded by a farm community. The trains running down Main Street were not a tourist attraction in those years but accepted and tolerated for interrupting a lazy summer day when we counted the cars that went by or put nickels on the tracks. The train engineer always waved and sometimes pulled the whistle.

I was raised before Interstate 71 interfered with daily life after its opening in 1969. Shopping local was the only choice, and trips to "town" like Louisville and Madison, Indiana, were once-a-month excursions. The grocery and hardware stores were on Main Street, along with mom-and-pop diners, banks, pool halls, automobile dealers and feed stores like Southern States.

Farm life was the same for most everyone. Dairies and beef cattle operations were common, and a twenty- to fifty-acre farm was considered small. Most kids were tied to local history from the graveyards found in their backyards of early settlers in Oldham County dating to the late 1700s. My brother and I played many hours on a stone fence that surrounded the graves of Moses and Cynthia Duncan, who arrived on our farm around 1810. Dotted among the inscribed stones were blank stones and rocks that we called "slave graves," but we had little understanding of Oldham County's role in slavery until recent research at the Oldham County History Center revealed an incredible slave culture in those early years.

Tobacco was the cash crop, and adults got bootlegged alcohol from either "the bottom" or the back of Rush Gatewood's drugstore. Local teenagers hung out in the wee hours of a Saturday night with local cops at Roberts Service Station in the middle of town.

Our schools were segregated, and on each trip from our farm into LaGrange, we passed the LaGrange Training School, which later historical research revealed as one of the important Rosenwald Schools. In the early twentieth century, Rosenwald Schools were supported by funds for Black students from the generosity of philanthropist Julius Rosenwald.

The main thing I have learned about history is the resilience of spirit. This book identifies the local "hidden" history of LaGrange and, most importantly, the stories of the Living Treasures who lived through twentieth-century LaGrange. They are people who reflect what we all want to have for our lives and the communities we live in: hope, justice, humanity, kindness and a great deal of humor.

Part I
How LaGrange Got Its Name

The Marquis de Lafayette

Called Lick Branch and then Crossroads, the name "LaGrange" was finally selected when the Marquis de Lafayette visited Oldham County on his Farewell Tour of the United States. In 1824, President James Monroe invited the Marquis de Lafayette to tour the United States, partly to instill the "Spirit of 1776" in the next generation of Americans and partly to celebrate the nation's fiftieth anniversary. One of the Marquis's stops was to visit with his old friend Commodore Richard Taylor, who lived on a bluff overlooking the Ohio River near Westport. The Commodore was the uncle of William Berry "Big Foot" Taylor, who donated the town parcel and courthouse square that became LaGrange. It was from the Marquis's visit to the Commodore's home that William Taylor met Lafayette.

During the Revolutionary War, Lafayette left his country of France to fight for the cause of freedom and democracy in the United States. Lafayette led troops under the command of George Washington and fought in several crucial battles, including the Battle of Brandywine and the Siege of Yorktown in Virginia. He returned to France after the war and pursued a political career championing the ideals of liberty that the American republic represented.

He helped write, with Thomas Jefferson's assistance, the Declaration of the Rights of Man and of the Citizen, which was inspired by the United States Declaration of Independence. He also advocated the end of slavery, in keeping with the philosophy of natural rights. Lafayette was an American

The grave site of Commodore Richard Taylor near Westport. The Commodore's nephew William Berry Taylor met the Marquis de Lafayette at the commodore's home. *Author's collection.*

hero and one of the last generals still alive from the Revolutionary War when he made more than 170 stops on his two visits to America in August–September 1824 and June 1825.

The schedule of the tour was mostly driven by commitments Lafayette had already made, especially to large cities like Boston, New York and Washington, D.C. As a result, he consistently declined invitations from smaller towns because of the lack of access in those times, such as poorly maintained roads. Despite this very brief and tightly scheduled tour, the Marquis made special arrangements to visit with his friend Commodore Richard Taylor.

The Marquis called on Commodore Taylor in the last year of Taylor's life, 1825. The Marquis and the Commodore had forged a true friendship in Yorktown during their active military careers. The Marquis spent two days in Louisville, May 12 and 13, 1825, and visited the Commodore at his home at Woodlawn in Oldham County. One of Taylor's granddaughters vividly remembered the visit and recounted, years later, Lafayette's visit and kind attention to her, a girl of thirteen at the time. It would have been during this time that William Berry Taylor attended the reception by his uncle given for the Marquis, which inspired William Berry Taylor to change the name of the frontier town of Crossroads to LaGrange, in honor of the Marquis's estate in France. Many streets, cities, counties and squares across the United States today are named after General Lafayette and his La Grange estate on the outskirts of Paris. Most of those names are a direct result of the momentous Farewell Tour.

THE WILLIAM BERRY TAYLOR FAMILY AND THEIR INFLUENCE IN THE REGION

The largest Oldham County land developers in the early 1800s come from the Taylor families. When William "Big Foot" Taylor (1765–1836) came to the area, so vast were the estates of Major Taylor that he was nicknamed "Big Foot Billy" because it was said he had "to have owned all the land he put his foot on." His large landholdings were the results of land trades, survey work and inherited Revolutionary War grants from his family.

William Berry Taylor moved to Kentucky in December 1796 and bought one thousand acres on Floyd's Fork in Shelby County, which later became part of Oldham County in 1824. Major Taylor built a temporary dwelling log house. A year later, he returned to Virginia, bringing back with him his wife, Susanna Harrison Gibson Taylor, and three slaves, a woman and two men. The party came by boat from Virginia to Maysville and from there rode the rest of the way on horseback. As the family settled, Major Taylor built a large, elegant brick house on his estate, close to the Oldham and Shelby County line. He also built quarters for some fifty or more slaves, among whom were blacksmiths, carpenters, shoemakers and house servants.

As a surveyor, Taylor received one-ninth of the lands he surveyed. Although most of his land was in Shelby County before Oldham was established, he helped to set the boundaries of Oldham County. His holdings were bisected by the north and south road from Frankfort to Westport and east to west from Louisville to New Castle. These roads intersected at a

Portrait of William Berry Taylor, who donated the land for LaGrange and the courthouse square. *Oldham County Historical Society*.

Girls at the public spring in LaGrange. Spring water and a central location were important attractions for the selection of LaGrange as the county seat. *Oldham County Historical Society*.

public spring, which eventually resulted in the settlement of the Crossroads that later was renamed LaGrange.

William Taylor built a log house near Fourth and Jefferson Streets in LaGrange that grew into a sizeable house of fourteen rooms. The style of the home was known as a four square with huge, outsized chimneys at the four corners of the house and porches on three sides. The back side of the house, the back dining room and kitchen opened out on a bricked area with a dairy and a well. Taylor gave the home to his daughter Elizabeth, who married Dr. John Willett of Shelbyville. Upon her death, Elizabeth willed the home to her niece Bettie Mallory (the granddaughter of William Berry). The home was razed in the 1930s to make way for the McCarty and Ricketts Funeral Home, and the building still stands today.

The Taylor Families

William Taylor's family was one of the most influential in American history. There is no doubt their influence directed American history and democracy both in their contributions in the Revolutionary War and its success as well and in political influences by producing two U.S. presidents, James Madison and Zachary Taylor. They also influenced the slave trade by their slave ownership, which cast a broad net as the family moved westward, bringing large numbers of enslaved laborers into our local region.

The Taylor family line that settled in Oldham County goes back to James Taylor Jr. (1675–1729) and his wife, Martha Thompson Taylor (1679–1762). Taylor's father was the first in the Taylor line to come from England. James Taylor was a companion of Governor Spotswood and one of the members of the Knights of the Golden Horseshoe in 1716. This land-surveying expedition, which crossed the Blue Ridge Mountains into the Shenandoah Valley, took possession of the land between the Blue Ridge and the ocean in the west in the name of King George I of England. Those who had been part of the expedition then began to stake out claims to the land that had been surveyed, James Taylor being among them.

James and Martha had nine children: Zachary (1707–1768), Frances (1700–1761), Martha (1701–1782), James (1703–1784), Mildred (d. 1790). George (1711–1792), Tabitha (1713–1794), Erasmus (1715–1794) and Hannah (d. 1762). James and Martha's children, grandchildren and great-grandchildren were in military and civil service, some serving in the Revolutionary War. Some of these children served as surveyors during the westward expansion that included Kentucky. Both as surveyors and military officers, they were awarded land grants.

James and Martha's great-grandson was James Madison, the fourth president of the United States. Another great-grandson was Zachary Taylor, twelfth president of the United States. Their sons Zachary (1707–1768) and George (1711–1792) are the two men that this book specifically targets because of their associations with the Taylors of Oldham County.

Zachary Taylor Sr. (1707–1768) had a son, Lieutenant Colonel Richard Lee Taylor (1744–1829), who produced President Zachary Taylor (1784–1850). Lieutenant Colonel Richard and his wife, Sally Strother Taylor, settled in Louisville with his family, bringing their infant son Zachary with them. Taylor settled his family on what was then a one-thousand-acre parcel of land and built the home Springfield, which became the boyhood home of our twelfth president, Zachary Taylor. Taylor also was married at Springfield, and he returned to the home many times during his adult life. The home today has been privately preserved and protected by Bill and Barbara Gist. The Zachary Taylor National Cemetery, off Brownsboro Road in Louisville, is essentially located in the backyard of Springfield, and President Taylor is buried there.

Zachary Taylor Sr.'s brother George had nine sons who fought in the Revolutionary War, eight of whom qualified for land grants in Kentucky. These included Lieutenant Jonathon Gibson Taylor and Commodore Richard Taylor (one of the sons died in the war). Lieutenant Jonathon Gibson Taylor was William Berry Taylor's father. Commodore Richard Taylor (1749–1825) brother of Jonathon, was William Berry Taylor's uncle. Five months prior to the Declaration of Independence, Commodore Taylor became an officer in Virginia's Colonial Navy. From his leadership, he quickly gained rank in the Revolutionary War, and by the end of the war, he was the designated commander of the entire naval fleet. He never lost a ship during his years when he served as captain.

The Commodore retired in 1789 and built the family a home known as Woodlawn on the Ohio River, about twenty miles east of Louisville, close to the towns of Westport and Goshen. He and his wife, Catherine Davis Taylor, had eleven children. The Taylor family also had one hundred enslaved laborers they brought with them in their move to Woodlawn. The Commodore built a fine two-story log home on high ground about a mile back from the river but with a view of it. The home is now gone, but from stories passed down, it was fashionable and comfortable for an active family life with young children.

Richard and Catherine were in their mid-forties when they settled in their Kentucky home, but their life was plagued with physical and financial woes. Lameness and chronic suffering continued to the end of Richard's life from the unhealed war wound in his knee. The year after Catherine's death in 1810 at age sixty, their daughter Matilda's husband was murdered, and the Commodore urged Matilda to come with her children—Richard, Eliza, Catherine and Mary Ann—to live with him. Richard passed away on August 30, 1825, at age seventy-six. He and his wife are buried on their farm, and the Commodore's grave has received a special Revolutionary War marker.

William Berry Taylor's nephew John Martin Taylor was another Taylor with large slaveholdings in Oldham County. The son of William's brother Samuel Mitchel Taylor (1785–1853) John Martin lived in Westport and had a ten-thousand-acre cotton plantation in Arkansas. John Martin met his wife, Mary Arnold, when she was visiting relatives in Kentucky. Mary's stepfather, Peter Rives, had large landholdings in Arkansas that later became the connection that resulted in the purchase of a cotton plantation in Arkansas that Taylor named Hollywood because of the massive holly trees growing on the estate.

Taylor built a very grand Italianate mansion on the banks of the Ohio River, near Westport, that he called Mauvilla. Taylor descendant Mrs. Dillard H. Saunders recalled that the nineteen-room Mauvilla mansion was built in

1855 from homemade brick made by slaves and had large high-ceiling rooms that opened into an immense hall that featured a large circular stairway. On the third floor of the mansion, half-story rooms were lit by smaller windows under the roof. A large cupola on the roof gave views of the immense landscape of the Ohio River Valley. The balcony had an iron balustrade opening from the second-story window. There was a large "avenue" that led from the house to the river. According to Saunders, pilots on the Ohio River said they steered their boats on the Cincinnati-to-Louisville run using Mauvilla as a landmark from any direction. There was also mention of a huge stone bathtub, weighing two tons, as an unusual feature of the house, earning it the title of the first bathroom fixture in Westport.

The Taylor family "commuted" back and forth between their Kentucky and Arkansas homes. According to Gould's research in Arkansas, Dr. Taylor had 184 slaves on his cotton plantation Hollywood, which made him one of the largest slaveholders in the state of Arkansas. Many of these enslaved laborers were from Oldham County.

In the 1860 census of Oldham County, one-third of the population was listed as enslaved laborers. Many of these laborers were part of the Taylor families who had inherited large land grants or served as surveyors, receiving land as a part of their service. By the end of the Civil War, enslavement had left a population of people who were seeking better lives and opportunities but with little assistance, education or money. Small towns like LaGrange offered some security to begin a new life.

Carlos McDowell, First Mayor, Dies in Tragic Fire

LaGrange made status as a sixth-class city by Kentucky statute by 1910, which required a mayor and six councilmen to be elected rather than operating through a board of trustees, as it had been since 1840. On May 12, 1910, Carlos McDowell was elected as the first mayor of LaGrange by the LaGrange City Council. McDowell replaced George W. Peak as mayor. Peak had been nominated, but it was determined that he was not eligible because he had not resided in LaGrange for one year. Unfortunately, McDowell only held the post for six months, as he died on December 15, 1910, while inspecting one of the many remains of buildings that had been lost that day to a large fire that swept through downtown LaGrange. His accident made headlines in the *Louisville Times* on December 15:

D.C. McDowell. Mayor of LaGrange was instantly killed by a falling chimney at 4:30 this morning while working in the ruins of last night's fire. He was assisting the Louisville fireman who came here in answer to a call for help. It had been decided to raze the chimney of Dr. Cassadys' residence one of the burned buildings in being regarded as a menace. Mayor McDowell had started to walk aways when the chimney collapsed, the top striking him on the head. His neck was broken, his arm fractured, and his shoulder crushed, death resulting instantly. Mayor McDowell was a druggist and one of the best-known residents of the city. He leaves a wife and son.

Carlos McDowell was the first mayor of LaGrange and died tragically during his first year in office. *Oldham County Historical Society.*

According to witness Captain Reese of the fire department:

McDowell was helping some of the boys to carry a line of hose around one of the buildings. This building had been practically burned to the ground and only a large chimney was standing. We had a line around it and intended to pull it down in a few minutes. Just about that time an L&N train went through the town at a rapid rate of speed and the chimney fell. McDowell was buried under a mass of bricks, and we had to dig him out. He was badly mangled and was dead before we got him out from under the bricks.

Fires in LaGrange

LaGrange was plagued by numerous fires throughout its early history because buildings were heated by coal and wood chimneys, which were often not inspected or cleaned properly. Fire alarms evolved over the years beginning with the bell at the Keynon Hotel, which was replaced by the courthouse bell.

The Louisville and Nashville Railroad helped put out fires by carrying tanks of water for firefighters to use. In 1895, when Colin A. Davies was made superintendent of the local division of the L&N Railroad, he presented

How LaGrange Got Its Name

This train rim on the courthouse lawn was originally used as a fire alarm during the turn of the twentieth century. *Author's collection.*

to the cities of Anchorage and LaGrange the rims from locomotive wheels. These were mounted in a frame, with LaGrange putting its in front of the courthouse. When the fire signal was to be given, sharp strikes with a small hammer made a sound that has been heard for ten miles.

The rim still stands in the LaGrange Courthouse lawn. Children used the rim for a nice swing that you could spin around, but in the last few years, a chain was placed to keep it intact.

Part II
LaGrange and the Train

History and Recollections

LaGrange history circumvents the establishment of the railroad, but in 1851, the train became the focus of LaGrange culture when tracks were laid down the center of Main Street. Imagine the difficulty of horse-and-buggy traffic when exposed to the roar of the steam engine and the shriek of the steam whistle for the first time. Ashes and cinders became a major cleaning problem for businesses and homes situated alongside the tracks until engines were gradually switched to diesel from the 1930s through the 1950s. Courthouse documents at the Oldham County History Center were covered in coal dust and had to be cleaned by volunteers. The first courthouse (circa 1827–73) in LaGrange had a fire in its cupola from sparks generated by the locomotive; this fire was put out before a second fire burned it down in 1873.

The Lexington and Ohio Railroad received its charter on January 27, 1830, from the Kentucky state legislature. The initial start began at Lexington and proceeded to the Ohio River as a direct route for goods and services. At the beginning, rail was painfully slow, both for track being laid and slow speed, traveling at fifteen miles per hour. But improved engines and better methods for clearing areas and laying track quickly progressed, and from 1850 to 1860, more than twelve railroad charters were granted to various lines. By the early 1850s, rail traffic was making its way through town.

There were various railroad spurs along the route through LaGrange that went into smaller communities in the area. The Louisville and

Frankfort route carried travelers through town and expanded in 1869 into the Louisville, Cincinnati and Railroad Co. A short line was established between LaGrange and Covington, which made LaGrange the junction town. This meant trains often stopped here for various repairs or exchange of mail and various freight. The Louisville and Nashville Railroad soon emerged as the dominant rail carrier during the Reconstruction era, and many L&N workers started to settle in LaGrange. A water tower was built, and the L&N Lake was established to replenish the boilers needed for the steam locomotives. LaGrange quickly became an important town for travelers, with hotels and taverns quickly rising to the occasion. During the Civil War, trains were often used to transport both Union and Confederate soldiers. Trains also served as a transport for freedom seekers on the Underground Railroad.

The Louisville and Nashville Railroad Depot (circa 1910) at 412 East Main Street replaced several earlier depots on this site. The building is one story but has a ramp that leads to the full-size basement, which had several functions, such as storage for luggage and other railroad equipment. There was both an indoor and outdoor ticket window and an indoor waiting room that was distinctly separated during segregation years. After passenger service was no longer available, the depot served several functions over the years. Today, it serves as the LaGrange Railroad Museum with static train cars that can be rented for events.

The train generated many stories and personal experiences for the people of LaGrange. The following are some captured by the Oldham County History Center through oral histories.

Hazel Henson White

In 1957, we moved to Oldham County. We moved to the Wrights' farm on Jericho Road. That is when I started school at LaGrange Elementary. Soon after, my parents finally bought a house on Kidwell Lane in 1959 off Jericho Road, right by the railroad tracks. There were still five of us at home, and we still shared bedrooms! Mine was in the hallway, which blocked the front door. But we did have running water and one bathroom. My brother Cecil joined the navy in 1959. He sent money home and helped with the mortgage. He met a girl there and never came back to live. He lives in Pennsylvania.

We had to walk across the railroad tracks every day to catch the bus, and it was so scary. We had to crawl over or under the train. We lived by the switch track, and that is where the trains all stopped. We would have to walk half

Above: This depot dates from 1910 and replaced earlier depots on this site. *Oldham County Historical Society.*

Right: The Park Hotel (no longer extant) was across the tracks from the train depot with a tunnel for convenience of the passengers. *Oldham County Historical Society.*

mile down the lane and catch the bus or crawl over and catch the bus, which was closer. That train would jump and jerk; we could have had our head cut off! I was little, and it was hard for me to crawl over the hitch. We would also climb on the ladder and hold on and catch a ride then jump off when it started picking up speed. Back then, there were a lot of hoboes. My mother would invite them in and fix them sandwiches and she would give them a quart jar with something to drink. Can't imagine doing that today!

Jimmy Roberts
My dad worked part time for Mr. Peak at Peak's Funeral Home, and sometimes on Sunday afternoons, the Peaks would go somewhere, and we would go up there and mind the phone. Aunt Ethel [Roberts] *and Lib Roberts were the phone operators; back then, you picked up the phone and say, "Auntie, get me one five!" For something to do, we would sit up on the balcony and count the hoboes as the trains went by. One time, we counted fifteen.*

We would go up to the depot sometimes for something to do in the summer. There was a "white only" water fountain at the depot, and the restrooms were segregated. We also went down to the L&N Lake and sometimes camped out there. Hoffman's Greenhouse was there on the L&N Lake. Jessie Joe and Beano would be down there.

Nancy Timmons
The trains running through LaGrange were our life. The trains reminded us there was an outside world, going to someplace and coming from someplace. I always lived close to the railroad tracks. Mother said when I was about one and a half years old, I had double pneumonia. Dr. Walsh fashioned an oxygen tent around me and found some drug to help me. She said they sent the drug out on the interurban train for him to use.

Many mornings when I woke up there were cinders on my sheets from the trains. I used to hitch a ride on the train as it went through town (very slowly!) to visit my friends. The train would often come to a complete stop. I would just jump on the ladder as it went through town. Margie Pollard was a real expert at that! I am not sure why the trains would stop; but they would stop forever. During the war, the train would come through with the soldiers—oh boy—the soldiers would throw letters to us to mail. The soldiers would come out here from Fort Knox, and they had dances for them in the gymnasium down by LaGrange High School. A lot of them were pilots, and then the next day they would fly over LaGrange and "buzz" us. I would say we probably had three or four weddings from those associations.

Girls posing on the track. *Left to right, front row*: Jean Rose Pierce Theiss, unknown, Geneva Ransdell, Nancy Cassady Doty, Mary Lou Bell and Sheryl Hess. *Standing in back*: Nancy Catlett Timmons. *Oldham County Historical Society.*

After I graduated from high school, Jean Dowell Taylor and I would ride the train home from Frankfort, where we both worked. Steam engines were so much friendlier than diesels.

Bob Arvin
When we moved back to LaGrange, my parents rented a couple of places, then they bought a house on Chestnut Street on Third Court, and we lived there until I was seven. As you go in the Courts, they have the concrete pillars at the end of the Court, and we would sit on the pillars and watch the trains across the street. They would pull up and put water in the engines. I can remember seeing hoboes, and I would see them all the time. The railroad track came right through my grandfather's farm [Raymond Arvin] *on Spann Lane. They would come up to the house and knock on the door and ask for something to eat, and Mother would fix them a sandwich. That was not uncommon.*

Bobby Brown
After we moved to LaGrange, my brother and sister, Bill and Lynda, were born in 1946; they were twins. We lived in a duplex owned by my aunt Ruth located across from the train depot on Main Street. The mail was delivered to the depot by the L&N Railroad train; there was a man named

Bill who pulled a mail cart down from the depot to the post office. I would sit and watch the train, and at times as kids, we put pennies on the railroad tracks. We also saw hoboes on the train, sitting on the cars when the doors were open.

Diane Booker

My mom worked at night at Central State Hospital and my dad worked on the L&N Railroad during the day, and he farmed when he got off. We had to go do hay, and when it was tobacco time, I was the one that set the tobacco. He was on the railroad crew that went around and fixed rails. Dad always went up to the goat houses by the railroad. And I think they met in the shed behind the goat houses. They called them the goat houses; one of them is still there, across the tracks. It is on top of the hill, there across from the depot and the storage sheds. The goat houses were where the railroad workers stayed.

I had an aunt and uncle who lived in Frankfort, and I would catch the train during school break and stay with them. And we would catch the train to Eminence when they had a special Fourth of July. There was a big picnic at the fairgrounds, and they had dances and everything. I loved the trains. They would dress me up with a hat, and I would get on the train. My aunt fixed my hair in Shirley Temple curls, using a brown paper bag to roll my hair. She always made sure I had clean underwear on! I had a tag I wore around my neck, and they would sit you down and you stayed there. There was a dining car, but it was for whites only. I was in the separate car completely from the whites; there was the colored car and white car. And that is the way they had the train station too; we had to go around the side and didn't board where the whites boarded.

The annual Fourth of July event at Eminence was big. They had lodges that sold food and bands playing and games for people; it was a fun day. My aunt and uncle lived right at the edge of Eminence. The train dropped people off at the fairgrounds. There were so many people.

Flo Lewis

There was a train, then, that came from Eminence to LaGrange. My grandmother Cora Louden lived in Eminence. That was my momma's momma. Lots of time, she would catch the train in Eminence and the conductor knew her. Instead of taking her to LaGrange, the conductor would make a stop at our house and we would see Granny get off the train and go meet her.

Al Klingenfus

Hardest times was in the '30s, when they were having the Dust Bowl out west. We had a drought, and it got down to a little bit of water; we had to depend on the spring. We would have to put in big tubs to collect the water during the day because sometimes the spring almost dried up. It got so bad that when there was a fire in Crestwood, the L&N Railroad would have to bring out water. And it was hard times. Didn't have any equipment like now; did everything with horses.

Ruby Duncan

I think it was about 1936 when I was a little girl and rode the train to Winchester to be with my father and relatives. I would stand at the LaGrange depot and wait for the train to come chugging in. Mother would pin a note on my dress with a big safety pin, and it had my name and destination written on it. She would say, "Now don't buy any apples from the man that sells them on the train. He spits on the apples and then polishes them to make them shine. And don't buy a sandwich from the people in Frankfort that sells them through the window of the train. Who know who made them; they may make you sick." I didn't buy the apples or the sandwiches, and I arrived in Winchester with my little bit of money in my pocket. The train had a cattle car way back next to the caboose. The windows were open. You got a lot of cinders in your eyes.

Harry Booker

I worked on the railroad too, in LaGrange, for about four or five years. Back in that time, they had section hands—kept the railroad up. Tap [railroad] *ties, all the cinders come out of the small boxcar, and you'd go up there and dump it all out and put the cinders under the crossties. You take a shovel around the ties and tapped the ties. You'd put a shovel under the ties and put cinders under the ties.*

Nancy Doty

And I remember when the troop trains would come through and we would all go out and stand on the street and wait for the soldiers, and sometimes it would go real slow, and they would have mail and they would hand us letters and ask us to take them to the post office.

We would be sitting in Mary Dee's and hear the trains coming, and we would just go out and check to see if it was a troop or not, and a lot of them were passenger trains, and that was the days of the old steam engines....

And so when you went out you would get cinders all over your face and hair. That was in the old days before the diesel and all that stuff came out.

Mabel Tingle
During that time, it was World War II. I remember going to LaGrange, and all the troops would be on the train going to LaGrange. They would throw their names and addresses out, and I wrote to one. He was stationed I think in Arkansas; I don't know what happened to him. You wouldn't know when the troops would come through.

Nancy Oglesby
We would ride the train to Cincinnati to the zoo. Every once in a while, they would have special excursions with a special ticket to go to Cincinnati.

I also remember that the train turned over several times in LaGrange. My teacher had a brother, and he was trying to jump on the train to ride it through town, and he got both legs cut off. We also had a lot of hoboes back then. They always said they mark your house, a pole near your house, if you give food. We always had them; she [mother] always fixed them a sandwich and put it in a sack. She never had them in; a lot of people did. One time a hobo came into our house when we were having dinner. Dad and my brother were there. When she asked them in, she realized he had been drinking. My dad and brother got him out. There were empty cars, over across from the courts, and they would live there. They would come over and ask Mother for needle and thread too. Further up the road on Highway 146, there was an airport, on the left. Somewhere between there and town there were gypsies that would camp out. When an airplane would land, we would run up there to see it!

Jimmy Oldson's Barber Shop was on the section of Main Street where the railroad track slightly curves, resulting in accidents, as Jimmy recalled: "Every Derby Day, we would have to go out on that train track and help people get their cars off the railroad track. People would run their cars off on the tracks; they didn't realize the road ended."

The Interurban Railroad

The Louisville and Eastern Electric Railroad, also called the interurban, was a one-car passenger trolley that ran by an electric cable overhead connected by wooden poles. It could seat up to forty passengers, and the engine was driven by the conductor. The back part of the passenger seats on the car could flip so passengers could always face forward because it was difficult to back up the trolley. When it reached the destination, the conductor drove the trolley around a small circle and flipped the seats, and passengers would be facing forward. The interurban was extended to LaGrange in 1906 and made its turnaround behind the interurban depot, near the corner of Second and Main Streets. Al Klingenfus remembers the stories about the interurban's construction from his dad and uncle:

> *One of my uncles was a motorman* [for the interurban]. *He lived with my grandparents. He told me when they built the interurban line, they didn't know what they were going to name these little stops, so a couple of guys rode the car and they were naming all the stops: Buckner, Beard's Station and so forth.*
>
> *Originally, the interurban ran from Louisville to Crestwood, and* [the railroad] *decided it was so profitable they would extend the line to LaGrange. That made L&N Railroad mad because a lot of people rode railroad cars in those days* [and they were afraid to lose business]. *So they complained about the interurban going in. So they* [the interurban] *thought the best way to do it was to lay the tracks at night. So, the L&N Railroad men tried to pull the track. They shot steam on the workers* [who] *were laying the interurban tracks. So, the L&I* [Louisville and Interurban] *streetcar company put electric on the railroad line. The rail and the whole bunch just fell down. It didn't kill them, but it shocked them so. My dad told me that he remembered that. You can see why they would do it; they were trying to come to LaGrange, and L&N would try to stop them. Dad was there. After shooting that hot water on them, they got them back.*

The following is an example of an interurban timetable from the Oldham County History Center Collection:

> *Time Table effective May 17, 1925*
> *Trains leave LaGrange for Louisville and way stations daily at 5:35, 6:32 a.m. then hourly from 7.35 a.m. to 9:35 p.m. then 11:15 p.m. Additional trains daily except Saturday, Sunday and holidays at 7:05 p.m. Express trains leave LaGrange daily at 7:00 a.m. and daily except Sunday and holidays at 2:00 p.m.*

The interurban electric train depot (no longer extant) at the corner of Second and Main provided daily train service to Louisville from 6:00 a.m. until midnight. *Oldham County Historical Society*.

J.W. Hall remembers riding the interurban regularly as a boy:

> *I used the streetcar from LaGrange to Crestwood. We would get off to the Stoess's Sweet Shop and Hardware Store, and Mr. Stoess would give us a peppermint ball every morning when we got off to go to school. I remember coming to LaGrange* [on the trolley], *and there was always a group of youngsters who would like to pull the trolley. The conductor would go out and pull the rope around the turntable and turn the car around to go back toward Louisville. About the time he got in there, they* [the youngsters] *would go pull the rope off the electric coming in the trolley car, and he would have to get back off and run them off and start over.*
>
> *The seats were leather, and it was nice. The trolley ran on time. My parents let me go on the trolley and think nothing about it.*

A lot of locals took advantage of the interurban for commuting to Louisville for work and school. David Monroe recollected:

I used to go to U of L with some of the workers at Belknap. That was at First and Main, and I would walk over to Third and Main, pick up the trolley car and ride the trolley to Gardener Inn and walk right in to Gardner Hall. Martha Manby rode with her friends. Mary Pryor went in to U of L to school and took the interurban. I remember going with her several times. I can't remember where all the stops were.

There were also tourist attractions that developed around the interurban in LaGrange to draw people from Louisville out to the country air. A resort was built in the early 1900s on the Anita Springs property, at the end of Kentucky Street, called the Royal Inn, Magnesia Springs Station, to take advantage of the interurban electric train and L&N Railroad.

The interurban lost its appeal during the Depression years with the advent of the automobile and shut down in 1935. The interurban depot served many functions over the years, such as an antique store, restaurant and bakery for commercial pies. It was torn down in the 1980s, when the DeHaven Baptist Church made the site into a parking lot.

Part III
The Schools

LaGrange Grade and High School: Origins from Funk Seminary Masonic College

Early in the area's history, LaGrange and Oldham County citizens were interested in providing educational opportunities for their children. In 1838, Kentucky set aside $1 million for a permanent school fund. Oldham County citizens followed action and voted 652 to 208 for a school tax of two cents on $100 of taxable property. This made history in the state of Kentucky. One of Oldham County's citizens, William Funk, who died in September 1841, set aside $10,000 to establish an educational facility to be called Funk Seminary. Construction of the seminary was barely completed when, in 1844, the Grand Lodge of Kentucky took Funk Seminary and changed the name to the Kentucky Masonic College in 1846. By that time, there were 203 students, male and female, enrolled in the college. Students from out of town boarded with families. At one time, the Barbour home on Washington Street served as a dormitory for girls.

The site chosen was composed of four lots behind the public square in LaGrange and cost $350. The building was completed in 1843 and described as a substantial and commodious college edifice, measuring fifty by sixty-five feet, two stories high with eight rooms. The brick building cost $4,500 to build, and its edifice was supported by a pedimented gable supported by four large columns, forming a vestibule. The school was managed by the Grand Lodge to be established "and endowed at the expense of the Grand

Originally the Funk Seminary, this educational facility became the Kentucky Masonic College, attracting students from surrounding states until the Civil War led to its demise. *Oldham County Historical Society*.

Lodge and at which they might educate the orphans of Masonry on the labor principle by teaching them to practice healthy labor and mechanical arts in addition to the useful branches and English education."

The first session of the school opened on the first Monday of November 1844, with a primary department for "reading, writing, 'orthography,' arithmetic, geography and grammar." In the senior department, the course of study was "science, literature, Latin and Greek," with French and Spanish extra. Citizens of LaGrange and Oldham County would be permitted to send their sons as "pay students," with annual tuition being six dollars for primary students and ten dollars for higher department.

By 1848, a female school at LaGrange had also voluntarily come under Grand Lodge control. Total enrollment was in excess of 170 students (including charity students from twelve lodges), and the name had changed to the Masonic Seminary and Masonic College. Through the diligent efforts of the Grand Lodge of Kentucky, the state legislature in 1850 deemed it appropriate to confer on the college the full rights and privileges of a university. It was at that time that the name was changed to the Masonic University of Kentucky, and the Grand Lodge of Kentucky appropriated $1,000 for the education of female children of deceased Master Masons.

W.C. Barrickman wrote that during one of the Christmas holidays during the school's earlier years, students decided that the "pedimented" gable was not adequately ornamental, so they "borrowed" a nice red farm wagon, took it apart and carefully and laboriously reassembled it astride the building's ridge top.

During the period from 1850 to 1861, the university made decided headway and progress, growing to full re-enrollment and enjoying a reputation for sound scholarship. The school boasted it had students from Kentucky, Missouri, Tennessee, Mississippi and Louisiana. This came to a sudden end in 1861 with the outbreak of the Civil War. The student body quickly disintegrated over the Civil War years, and the faculty gradually dissolved. The strain of the Reconstruction period drained the essential funding needed from the Grand Lodge. On May 1, 1873, the Masonic University of Kentucky ceased to exist, and the Grand Lodge turned back the property and school equipment to the trustees, according to the will and testament of William Funk.

The school returned to a high school status and continued to operate as Funk Seminary, charging tuition and offering classes. Graduation exercises were often held on the second floor of the Sauer Building on Main Street. The building burned to the ground on the night of September 24, 1911. Rumors had it that the fire was accidentally set by gamblers who were said to have used the cupola of the building for "surreptitious" games.

Work was begun on a new school that was called Funk Seminary and included elementary and high school grades, but the location was moved west on Jefferson Street from the original site (which is LaGrange Elementary School today). According to the 1926 anniversary edition of the *Oldham Era*, the new school was built on the site of a slave cemetery. The property was part of the original William Berry Taylor plat. The Taylor home, which was razed for the Radcliffe Funeral Home in 1937, included a large farm area. William Berry Taylor gave the home and site to his daughter Elizabeth

LaGrange Grade and High School opened doors in 1911. Today, it is the site of the LaGrange Elementary School. *Oldham County Historical Society*.

and her husband, Dr. Sam Willett, who were slaveholders. The bodies were exhumed and reinterred in the Historic African American Cemetery at the intersection of Third and Fourth Streets.

The new school contained four classrooms downstairs, besides the office, library and large auditorium. There were four classrooms upstairs and a laboratory. There was a large basement, one room of which was equipped for manual training. By 1919, enrollment had increased to such an extent that it was necessary to have more room. In 1920, the PTA built three classrooms and a domestic science room in the basement. More bodies were found when digging in the basement to fit the classroom, and these were also moved to the African American cemetery. The first session in the new school opened in January 1912 with an enrollment of 250, while enrollment for 1921 was 404.

A gymnasium was added in 1922 through donations and subscriptions from local citizens. The gym was ninety feet long and sixty feet wide of steel frame construction and included electric lighting and heat from furnaces. During the winter months, it became a place for basketball games, roller skating and other recreation. Throughout the next few decades, the gymnasium hosted many community events, including New Year's Eve and

A float waiting for the Jones Downey Parade on September 26, 1953, by the old gymnasium on Fifth Street at the LaGrange Grade and High School. *Oldham County Historical Society.*

The Schools

Valentine dances. The gymnasium burned to the ground in 1960 from a fire caused by an antiquated furnace.

One of the most memorable teachers at LaGrange was Mamie Goldsborough, who is mentioned several times in the following interviews from her students during the 1930s.

Ruby Duncan

My first-grade teacher was Miss Mamie Goldsborough. Miss Mamie wore long black skirts and high button shoes, a white apron over the skirt and long-sleeved white Victorian blouses. She had a cot at the back of the room. If you were sick, she would put you to bed, give you an aspirin, take your temperature and put a whiff of smelling salts under your nose. It seemed to work! We all made it through.

A little wall ran around the room. You stood on that to write on the blackboard, and if you were naughty, you were made to stand with your back to the room on that wall. Miss Mamie pointed to each word in your reading book with a knitting needle. If you didn't know the word, you got a rapping on your hands with the knitting needle or a ruler. I never did get my hand spanked. I knew those words!

Miss Mamie made her own paste and put a little bit in seashells and passed them around for pasting pictures in our little art class. It smelled so good you wanted to eat it! She would wash the shells in a bucket of water to have them cleaned for another day. Miss Christine was Miss Mamie's sister. She wrote the social column for the Oldham Era. *She wore the long black skirts and high button shoes, too, and carried an umbrella and a large satchel. She played piano and organ.*

My favorite teacher was Mrs. Bernice Maddox Fendley. She was my fourth-grade teacher. Her son is John Fendley, our county attorney now. My daughter, Mary Ann, also had Mrs. Fendley as her teacher when she attended grade school, and Mrs. Fendley was one of her favorite teachers, too.

In 1937, the big flood came. People in Louisville were in so much need. They brought people out here and used our school for refugees. We were out of school for some time. When we went back to school, the floors that were wooden had been oiled and the school had been fumigated. My aunt that lived in Louisville walked a pontoon bridge with her family to get to safety. They came and stayed a while with us.

The old gym was the place for fun. The Halloween parties in the 1930s were wonderful, I thought. Homemade candy and cakes, popcorn balls, cider. They formed a line and did the cake walk around the gym to pick the best costume. We also roller skated in the gym. You got the skates as you went in the door, and you used a key to clamp them on your shoes. The skates had wooden wheels.

We had our senior prom in the old gym. It was wartime, and you did the best you could with what you had. Dan Bland was the leader of that event, and we turned the old gym into a beautiful flower garden. I think the prison band played for the prom. It seems there might have been about eight members in the band. I think they wore matching white coats. I have no pictures of the prom.

Dot Smith
One of my good friends was Virginia Singer, who lived next door to the Goldsborough sisters, Mamie and Christine. (Mamie was my schoolteacher.) I remember when I began my first-grade school, I had to walk to school, and Miss Mamie would come by my house every morning in her long dark skirts and big black bag and walk me to school.

When Miss Mamie found out I was left-handed, she would hold my hand out and hit it with a ruler. She did not believe I should be left-handed, and she really tried to change me. She would do that every day, and I didn't tell Mom about it. All my other teachers were nice, and I loved school and learning. We would start class with a Bible verse, pledge to allegiance and a prayer. She was very religious.

I am not sure I can remember all my teachers, but I started with Miss Mamie Goldsborough, then Mary Russell, Rose E. Smith, Ollie K. Smith, Elizabeth McMakin, Doris Welch, Pine Isaacs, Lloyd Moody, Verna Radcliffe, Naomi Smith, Mary E. Snyder and Nena Sparks. H.R. Kirk was principal until my senior year, then Mr. Baker. All of the grades through high school were in that one building at LaGrange (same location where LaGrange Elementary is located today). There was a third floor in the old building, and that was the high school. There wasn't a lunchroom when I went there; everyone brought their lunch to school.

Nancy Timmons
I went to LaGrange Grade School and High School—spent a lot of time with my nose in a circle! I had Miss Mamie Goldsborough for one of my teachers. I was rambunctious, but she and Mr. Kirk pretty well took care of me. I remember we had a picture, next to George Washington, of Frances Willard. She was the Loyal Temperance Team leader; I do think she must have started Prohibition. Well, I had a nice loud singing voice, so I was

The Schools

selected to lead the Temperance Parade and march down Main Street. We all wore the little white ribbon that meant "temperance." The words were "When asked to drink I will smile and turn my glass upside down!" to the tune of "Auld Lang Syne."

The Wedding of the Painted Dolls was a play we put on at LaGrange Elementary. We had a great play every year. Doris Welch Cassady directed it, and Mildred Guthrie played the piano.

A lot of events took place in the gymnasium, as remembered by the following from oral history interviews.

Johnny Glauber

The old gym at LaGrange was all wood construction and four rows of bleachers on the side and heated by a big coal furnace. The furnace was down in the basement, and the vents were right at the score table. The basement was just big enough for the furnace to sit down in there. They had a regular basketball season there, and then in the summertime, LaGrange started a recreation program for kids. They would have basketball and table

LaGrange High School band in the old gymnasium with music teacher Guy Ashmore, 1952–53. *Oldham County Historical Society.*

tennis, and at night, they used it for a roller rink. Mr. John Oechsner took care of that, and he was the basketball coach. They had a huge New Year's dance there every year. The night it burned down was before a New Year's Eve dance. There was a default in the furnace.

The Kentucky State Reformatory orchestra played at the New Year's Eve dance. They were called The Stardusters. It was composed of fifteen or twenty inmates. Sponsors would decorate the gym up real good. (Nancy Doty recalled that they paid the inmates that played in the band with a carton of cigarettes!)

They used to have donkey basketball games in the basketball courts! And then one of the tallest men I ever saw came to town as a part of a traveling team, like the Globetrotters, but it wasn't as well known. He could almost actually reach up and grab the goal. They billed him as one of the tallest men in the world! Our fire department sponsored a couple of circuses that came to town.

JIMMY ROBERTS
I went to LaGrange when the old gymnasium was still there. I was the manager of the basketball team for Mr. Hehl. And for a while, they also roller skated in the gym. A lot of parents helped to maintain things at the gym, like the PA system. I helped people with their skates. I would help tighten the clamps on their shoes. I got to skate free! They didn't charge much. They used the gym in the summertime for roller skating. Then after the summer, Mr. Larberger would come in with Norman Hall, his son-in-law, and sand the floors to get it ready for the fall.

During the segregation years (before 1964), Blacks could use the gyms on Saturday. Harry Booker was one of those ballplayers. You couldn't play basketball in LaGrange [in the gym]—*only on Saturdays* [if you were Black]. *Professor John Trapp would let Negro boys come down to the gym and play in LaGrange. He would say, "You gonna play, you gonna do it right." He was a hardnose coach. Me and Speedmore went down there, and Professor Trapp whopped me and Speedmore together* [at basketball]. *Me and Speedmore get down there late at the gym, Professor Trapp said, "Do fifty laps around the gym." He was hardnose, but he was a good man. He was a principal for Oldham County Schools, and he was a basketball coach.*

HERBIE HENDRON
I went to LaGrange Elementary, and my first teacher was Mrs. Hisle. I would ride my bike to school; it was a real nice school. They had a nice gym,

a merry-go-round. I would make Mrs. Hisle mad because I never would do my homework. I got a spanking from her and my parents. Mr. Flener was principal. One day, I was shooting paper clips with rubber bands—must have had two hundred to three hundred rubber bands in my pocket. And my buddy said, "Let me shoot 'em," and he shot someone in the head with one. So then I got called in to Mr. Flener's office. I was in the back room, and he asked me if I had any more paper clips on me, and I said, "No sir." And of course, I had a whole box in my pocket, and I thought, "Oh God, I done messed up" and about that time Mrs. Monroe walked in the office and said, "Mr. Fleener, you are wanted on the phone, it's urgent." And while he was gone, I emptied my pocket in his trash can and covered it with paper. When he came back, he said, "If I find any paper clips I am going to wear you out with that paddle!" I thought "whew." That paddle was in his office, and that thing looked like it was two feet long. It was six inches square, and the handle was curved so he could get a good grip. And he had three big holes drilled near the center; the holes were the size of a golf ball. And when he hit you, **POW***, and he wouldn't stop at one. One time he gave me ten or twelve licks and they weren't too bad, but that last lick, he snapped his wrist and let you have it.*

Miss Mary Russell was my third-grade teacher, and that was the year I got in the most trouble. I got 118 licks that year for not doing my homework. She said that I was the hard-headest boy she had ever seen. She had fingernails, must have been two inches long, and she grabbed me by the hair one day because I didn't do my arithmetic and had me in front of the blackboard and she said, "You answer these problems," and she hit me with that paddle, and I was spitting the answers out—and I don't know where the answers where coming from. And then when I got home, she had called my mother and I got it again. I was still crying when I got home, and I told my dad, "Take me up to the barbershop and get me a burr," and I had my head skinned. Went back to school the next day, and she said, "You got your hair cut off," and I said, "Yeah, and you can't pull my hair no more either!" I saw her twenty-five years later, when I was delivering mail at Weible's Beauty Parlor, and she said, "You still remember that?" and we both laughed.

After the old gym burned, a new gym was built as an extension to the school. It opened in 1960 and is still used by students at LaGrange Elementary. The auditorium in the LaGrange Grade and High School was a focus of many community events. It had an upper balcony and could seat

The large auditorium at LaGrange Grade School was a favorite venue for plays and skits produced by teacher Doris Cassady and her sister Edith Walsh, circa 1953. *Oldham County Historical Society*.

several hundred students. Large velveteen curtains and drapes squared the wooden stage, which had dressing rooms on each side. There were plays, dance recitals, school gatherings and many public events, such as 4-H talent shows. As a graduate of LaGrange Elementary, I remember our classes gathered to view science films hosted by Dr. Frank Baxter for the Bell System Science Series. *Our Mr. Sun*, my favorite, indicated the world would be solar powered by 2000. These films were free to public schools across the United States, and our school took advantage of them. I was excited about watching them when they came to school because they made the future world look so exciting. There were eight films that were produced in this series, which had reached six million schoolchildren by the mid-1960s.

In 1953, Oldham County High School opened its doors. This move consolidated the high schools from LaGrange, Liberty and Crestwood. A new annex was built on the older part of the building for elementary students, and seventh- and eighth-grade classes were held in the original structure. In 1966, the last eighth-grade class graduated from LaGrange, and a new junior high opened by Oldham County High School. The old building burned in 1980, but the annex was saved. A new replacement, with a library, offices and classrooms that connect the gym with the older annex, still serves the community today.

The LaGrange Training School: A Rosenwald School

The First Baptist Church, located at 419 North First Street in LaGrange, currently resides on the site of the LaGrange Training School, which was a school for African American children before integration of schools with the Civil Rights Act of 1964. The school was built in 1921 with a $1,000 grant from the Rosenwald Fund, which was matched with funds raised by the local African American community. The general public contributed remaining funds as well as local tax dollars to build the three-room schoolhouse that cost $6,600.

The LaGrange Training School was not the first site, however, for the education of LaGrange's Black children. By the end of the Civil War, local churches were an important place for Black children to receive an education. In LaGrange, the First Baptist Church and Kynett Methodist Church were sites for education classes. Elijah Marrs (1840–1910) was a preacher, writer and educator born into slavery who escaped and joined the Union army at the Taylor Barracks in Louisville. He also recruited local slaves to join the Union. After the war, Elijah moved around the area, mainly LaGrange, Eminence and Shelbyville, where he and his brother H.C. Marrs taught school for Black children, using funds from the Freedmen's Bureau. Marrs wrote about his experiences while in LaGrange:

> *During my four years residence in LaGrange, I made many friends. Among those I valued most highly were Elder Warren Lewis; Moses Berry, a former pupil and now a teacher in of the public schools of Missouri; Frank James; Salathiel Berry; Susan Davis; Mrs. Berry; Alice James; Josie Sutton; Annie and William Wilson; Eliza Barber; Caroline, Washington and Mary Bullitt; Mrs. Annie Lewis; and a host of others. Of Elder Warren Lewis, I can say much in commendation. When I was at his house, I received every courtesy, and nothing was too good for me. Elder Lewis, his wife and Susan Davis presented to my wife and myself a beautiful*

The LaGrange Training School (no longer extant) that served African American students until segregation ended in 1964. The school was created in the 1920s from Rosenwald funds. *Oldham County Historical Society*.

> *bouquet on our wedding day....During my career as teacher in LaGrange, I had under my supervision, at different times, three hundred children, and when I left there it was with the consciousness of having done my duty as a Christian and a teacher.*

The large number of students that Marrs discussed in his autobiography as having taught in LaGrange bear out numbers from the Kentucky State Census Report for Oldham County Schools. The 1900–01 list for Black children in LaGrange includes approximately 151 school-aged children. Parents listed for the children are George Carr, Mary W. Browning, Curtis Hinkle, Dr. R.B. Cassady, P.J. Gorham, Dan More, Boon Gipson, Alf Lawe, Will Bluford, Pete Wheeler, Jeff Thomas, W.H. Thomas, George Long, Henry Lee, Tishie Taylor, John Sutton, Spense Miller, Rose White, Jack Posey, Malinda Fible, Andy Todd, Tom Lee, Sue Sutton, William Dunbar, Hattie Watkins, Jack Sweeny, Ben Browning, Lila Coons, William Cushenberry, Henry Thomas, W.H. Bloomer, D.H. Bloomer, Lucy Green,

The Schools

Amanda Smith, Milton Taylor, Jerry Bibbs, Millie Taylor, Rena Beard, Jonas Smith, Pete Johnson, Slalie J. Newman, Charley Taylor, Henry Taylor, Lila Coons, Amanda Johnson, Tom Parrott, Maria Gipson, Ed Johnson, Square Shipman, John T. Taylor, Ed Young, John Van Cleave, Alex Beaumont, West Miller, John Doleman, Bettie M. Taylor, J.Q. Taylor, Mae Mason, Joe Davie, Dick Bluford, Eliza Davis, Mary Browning, George Buckner, Henry Barbour, Ben Elzie, Jane Foree, Tome Harris and Mary White. A complete list of the children with their parents can be found in the J.C. Barnett Archives and Library at the Oldham County History Center.

In 1874, the Kentucky General Assembly provided that a system of education be organized for Black children. In 1875, fifty cents was declared as set aside for each Black child whose name was on the school census.

In the Common School Report from the Superintendent of Public Instruction for Kentucky on June 30, 1893, there are twenty schools listed for white students in Oldham County and four schoolhouses listed for "colored" students. In the 1896 report, Superintendent J.L. Reeves noted that Oldham County spent $22,891 for white schools and $1,532 for "colored" schools. There were twenty-one schools for white children and eight schools listed for "colored."

Emma Laura Johnson (1911–2012) remembered the first Black school in LaGrange was a house near First Street and Washington. The archive records show the deed for this school was sold by Peyton Samuel Head on February 22, 1988, to William Whitlock, John Swinney and Abe Curtis as trustees of the Colored School District. The description from the deed marks the location: "Known as the Terhune property and bounded on the north by Washington street on the south by lot of Boston Baldack, in the east by an alley, on the west by 2nd Street located near what is known as the Public Spring."

The 1926 anniversary edition of the *Oldham Era* stated the school was an old house that was first occupied by the Terhune family, who were almost wiped out by cholera in 1873. The following is an article published on May 7, 1903, in the local *New Era* newspaper that validated the early organized efforts of the local Black teachers:

> *Colored Teachers Institute*
> *Interesting Meeting and Several Resolutions Adopted*
> *The Oldham County Colored Teacher's Institute opened its session Monday morning, August 10. Quite an instructive and interesting session was held with Mrs. Lillian Jones Brown, of Indianapolis, as instructor.*

> *Miss Lucy Blakemore, county superintendent, expressed herself as being very much pleased with the work of the institute and spoke many encouraging words to the teachers. Before adjournment the following resolutions were read and adopted:*
>
> *Whereas the pastor and trustees of Kynett M.E. church so cordially extended us the use of the church,*
>
> *Be it resolved That we tender them our thanks for the same.*
>
> *Be it further resolved, That we extend our thanks to Miss Mattie Blackstone for her efficient services as secretary during this session.*
>
> *Resolved That we extend our thanks to Miss Minnie Crutchfield o the Louisville Public Schools for her very material instruction in primary number work.*
>
> *Whereas Mrs. Lillian J. Brown, our instructor, so ably presented the various subjects,*
>
> *Be it further resolved That we tender her our hearty thanks.*
>
> *To Miss Lucy Blakemore, our worthy superintendent, we desire to show our appreciation of her untiring work and many kind words by giving better service in our several schools this year.*
>
> *Mrs. Bessie C. Jones*
> *Mrs. Bessie E Posey*
> *Mrs. Lavinia B. Gipson*

Cora Bullitt was the first Black student to pass the public school exam to go to high school. Her father, Washington Bullitt, a local leader, was a friend of Elijah Marrs in the early years of educational efforts and supported her desire to attend high school. At the time, there were two choices: Cora could take the train into Louisville to attend Central High School or go to Lincoln Institute in Shelbyville and stay in the dormitories during the week. Because her mother, Mary, was convalescent, Cora went to Central. Cora's brother John attended Lincoln Institute.

Emma Laura Johnson was another Black student in LaGrange who passed the public exam and went to Central High School on the train. She recalled:

> *We enjoyed the train. There were more than me that took the train; they came from Pleasureville and Jericho, Sarah, Florence Reed and Dolly Reed. We enjoyed the train, getting to ride. The only thing is you had to get up so early, 7 o'clock. We got off at the big station, off Broadway. Central wasn't that far from the station. Sometimes they would meet us if the weather was bad. I know we would get back about 7 at night....I thought*

Central was a good school. There was lot of kids there. They would brag on us; they said we were so smart. The principal said we were best behaved and had better people or something. I was sorry when I left [about 1929].

We took algebra, Latin, history. They had football [at Central]. *We didn't* [get] *a chance to get in many activities cause we had to catch the train to come back home. Sometimes we did our lessons on the train. There wasn't too much available, work like, after school. After I graduated, the most thing I ever done was domestic work, after my kids went to school.*

In 1921, the local LaGrange community raised a $1,000 matching grant for a new school, the LaGrange Training School, located at 419 North First Street. The Rosenwald Fund that supported the LaGrange Training School was established by Julius Rosenwald, part owner and president of the Sears, Roebuck and Company. A Rosenwald School was the name informally applied to over 5,300 schools, shops and teachers' homes in the United States that were constructed for the education of Black students in the early twentieth century. To promote collaboration between white and Black citizens, Rosenwald required communities to commit public funds to the schools and contribute additional cash donations. In Kentucky, 158 Rosenwald Schools and related educational buildings were constructed, including 12 training schools, between 1917 and 1932. Overall, the Rosenwald Fund donated over $70 million to public schools, colleges, universities, museums, Jewish charities and Black institutions before funds were depleted in 1948.

When the LaGrange Training School was finally constructed, it consisted of three classrooms, an auditorium and an industrial arts program. It had a couple of outhouses that were separate from the main building in the back of the two-acre lot. Later in the 1940s, the school obtained enough funds to put in a kitchen and a cafeteria.

The following are recollections from students who attended the LaGrange Training School.

Richard Reynolds

I went to LaGrange Training School. The teachers had grades one through four and then grades five through eight. My mother was my teacher from first through fourth grade. The older kids in the room helped teach the younger kids. We had to learn things that kids in school don't learn. We had to learn every state in the union, their capitals and capitals in major foreign countries. We had to recite the Gettysburg Address, poetry, Hamlet's soliloquy, the Preamble to the Constitution—we had to learn all that.

Class picture of teachers and students from the LaGrange Training School, circa 1950s. *Oldham County Historical Society.*

When the schools integrated, students from the Training School were ready to go to the white school.

We had two teachers from Jefferson County, and they had to take the motor coach from Louisville every day; they didn't drive. The teachers would bring movies about Blacks, like The Jackie Robinson Story, *and movies produced by Blacks. We learned about Black poets like Langston Hughes, Paul Laurence Dunbar. We had May Day every year with Pewee Valley School.*

DIANE BOOKER

The school had outdoor toilets and no running water, but there was a lunchroom. Mostly we carried our lunch, but I remember children making fun of our biscuits we had for lunch. I would bring a biscuit and meat or biscuit and apple butter, and Momma put in some kind of juice or water. My parents didn't have enough money for lunch money for four kids. I guess the kids made fun of us because we were poor, but I didn't think we were poor; I thought the biscuits were good!

There were three classrooms when I first started at LaGrange because there was a two-year high school, but after I was there about three years, the high school was no longer there, and you went to Lincoln Institute. So later there were just two rooms. There was a stage, and we had a piano for music, and they divided the rooms off with sliding doors. May Day was a big celebration each year. At the end of school, the Pewee Valley School and students from Lincoln Institute would come, and they would have baseball games and other different games to play, and then at the end of the day there would be the Maypole wrapping. You would be dressed up and get to wrap the Maypole; there were different color ribbons. We had a graduation from the eighth grade up at the Baptist church.

On occasion, if the students were well behaved, the faculty of the LaGrange Training School would take them on a field trip. This field trip consisted of a day trip to an area just up Highway 53 to a place called the County Lake. Here, students would play in Harrods's Creek and fish for crawdads and other wildlife. When the day was over, the kids would release their findings and return back to school, where they were then sent home.

We would also walk down to Mac's Lake with our teacher. We played in the water and collected crawdads and learned about different plants and animals. Miss Reynolds, Mrs. Gilbert, Mrs. Johnson and Mrs. Parrot were some of the teachers I remember.

Flo Thomas Lewis

I went to LaGrange Training School, and the bus picked us up where we lived on Jericho Road. I always wanted to learn, and I was so excited. My momma and several other ladies formed a group that now you would call the PTA. They would go to the school and help cook the lunches. People would bring in tomatoes and potatoes and stuff like that, people that lived on farms, would help feed the kids. My momma and the ladies would make sure the kids got lunch. There were several grades in each class. Grades one through five in one room and the sixth, seventh and eighth grade in another room. One teacher would teach all of us. At the end of the year, we had May Day, and everybody in the community would come. Then the next week, we had a play and made our costumes out of crepe paper. May Day was like a big field day: there would be a softball game, races and other games. There was always a pole, and we danced around the pole. You would invite your families; my aunties would come in from Eminence and Shelbyville. There would be tables, and people would bring cakes and they would make ice cream.

The LaGrange Training School was a center for local activities and published its own newspaper, the *Clarion*, which covered "LaGrange Training School and Vicinity News." In the May 1925 issue, subjects include a special auction by the PTA for ten cents a ticket of a beautiful chalk figure of a woman and the announcement of the Men's League to begin work on the foundation for the industrial building.

When the Civil Rights Act of 1964 was passed, outlawing segregation in the United States, students began attending LaGrange Elementary School and Oldham County High School in Buckner. Lincoln Institute closed its doors a few years later. The integration of whites and African Americans caused the school to shut down soon after.

A few years later, the empty schoolhouse was purchased and renovated into a new building for the First Baptist Church of LaGrange. The building was destroyed in a fire in 1990. The church rebuilt on top of the foundation of the previous building.

Part IV
The Oldham County Courthouse

The Beginning

When Oldham County was founded in 1824, the first Oldham County court cases were held in the home of George Varble at Lynchburg at the crossroads of Highway 53 and U.S. 42. Cases were moved to Westport at the home of Joel Kemper until the Westport Courthouse was constructed and held its first session on September 15, 1828. At the time, Westport was a vital shipping port with heavy commerce and trade from the Ohio River.

The early court documents contain papers signed by our first magistrates, sheriffs and justices of the peace (JOPC). One of the JOPC was William Gatewood, a slave owner who is documented through the narratives of abolitionist and slave Henry Bibb. Bibb is an international figure recognized for his leadership in the antislavery movement leading up to the Civil War. Gatewood enslaved Bibb and his wife and daughter.

As LaGrange was established in 1827, William Berry Taylor headed a group to move the county seat to LaGrange. Taylor donated land for the courthouse square in LaGrange, and a two-story brick courthouse was constructed on the square for the courthouse. There arose a community dispute over the shift of the county seat from Westport to LaGrange, and Westport retained the county seat temporarily until 1838. In 1838, the county seat was established permanently in LaGrange.

In those years between 1827 and 1838, church congregations held meetings in the courthouse in LaGrange. Often, conflicts on meeting dates

Above: The county seat began at Westport by the Ohio River in the original courthouse (circa 1828), which serves today as the Westport Methodist Church. *Author's collection.*

Opposite, top: This framed log courthouse in LaGrange first served local churches as a meeting place until the dispute was settled to move court from Westport to LaGrange. *Oldham County Historical Society.*

Opposite, bottom: James Mount, Oldham County jailor, and his wife, Amanda, lived in this home (circa 1840s) across from the courthouse square. It is part of the National Park Service Underground Railroad Network. *Author's collection.*

resulted between the Methodists, Baptists, Christians and Presbyterians. The churches eventually built their own structures, but they had permission to use the courthouse bell to call service. In the Court Order Book from 1846, the jailer was authorized to furnish the church groups the key to the courthouse to ring the bell.

During the years leading up to and through the Civil War, court documents include but are not limited to slave disputes over slave hire-outs and claims on runaways; unlawful liquor sales, including to slaves; estate settlements; illegal gambling; theft; abuse; harmful endangerment; deed disputes; property disputes; and murder. Slave auctions took place at the courthouse steps.

James Mount (1796–1864), who served as jailer, was responsible for holding runaway slaves until owners came to claim them, or if owners did not come, they would be sold through auctions. Money would go back to the county coffers for slave sales. James and Amanda Mount's house

The Oldham County Courthouse

at 106 North Second Avenue currently serves as the J.C. Barnett Library and Archives for the Oldham County History Center and is a designated site by the National Park Service on the National Underground Railroad Network. This is because of James's duties in holding and selling slaves as jailer, as well as the Mounts' slave ownership papers and bounty papers showing slave escapes.

An interesting court case during these early years was that of Bartlett Taylor. He was enslaved by the Jonathan Taylor family, and he grew up on their farm six miles north of LaGrange. At nineteen, he was sold to Berry and became a hire-out in Louisville, where he learned to be a butcher under Mr. Clisindoff. He saved $1,800 and fell in love and wanted to get married but not until he was a free man. Unfortunately, he lent his money out to some friends in need, but he wrote to his owner, Berry, expressing his wish to buy his freedom.

On September 20, 1840, Taylor went to the Oldham County Courthouse and was put on the auction block. He was sold for $2,000, himself being the highest bidder. Brent, the agent for sale, let Taylor make a promissory note for the $2,000, and Taylor, true to his promise, paid him back promptly. Taylor married Jane McCune of Abington, Virginia, as a free man.

Taylor became a very prominent citizen in Louisville, establishing a beef business and accumulating money and real estate. His wife died, and he married Miriam McGill. He had three daughters and one son. He became a founder of many churches throughout Kentucky and served as a missionary in both Kentucky and Tennessee.

The Civil War

Local LaGrange native Barbara Edds Calloway researched courthouse history when she began the Save the Courthouse group to try to stop the demolition of the 1875 structure in 2020. Through her research, she discovered a federal court claim, Doc. No. 1194, 63rd Congress, 3d Session, December 8, 1914, that awarded Oldham County $2,375 in full compensation for use and occupation of and damage to real estate by United States forces during the Civil War.

The document states that from December 1, 1864, through October 1, 1865, Union troops under the command of Colonel Buckley occupied the courthouse and courthouse yard. The troops listed included the 54th

Kentucky Mounted Infantry, a Michigan regiment and the 154th Ohio Infantry. Other war activities include telegraphs generated in LaGrange when Union troops were searching for John Hunt Morgan and his raiders as they were crossing the Ohio River.

> *On July 11, 1863, Burnside informed General Boyle that more troops were being sent to guard the Ohio River. "Colonel Sanders has arrived at Eminence. I have sent him the following orders: It is supposed that Morgan may attempt to cross the Ohio at either Westport, Grassy Flats, or opposite Bedford. Keep your scouts well out in the direction of Lockport, Port Royal, Bedford, and Westport. You can hire good citizen scouts and pay them well. Obey any orders General Boyle may send you. If Morgan attempts to cross at any one of these places you ought to whip him in detail. If he succeeds in crossing, he may try to cross Kentucky River between Carrollton and Lockport, and got out by Mount Sterling, in which case you must press him hard."…*
>
> *General Boyle telegraphed back to Burnside from LaGrange on the same day: "I am moving as fast as the artillery can go. We have marched since 9 o'clock last night. I am taking horses when necessary. I will be at the river by 10 p.m. Have sent scouts as directed."*

Fire Destroyed the Old Courthouse in 1873, Replaced by New Structure in 1875

According to former Oldham County judge Samuel DeHaven, "The courthouse was first struck by lightning and sometime afterward burnt. It caught in the cupola, presumably from a spark from a steam engine, at high noon. Nobody was sorry to see the old building go. We wanted a more up-to-date courthouse." Fortunately, the courthouse records were stored in a smaller brick building adjacent to the courthouse. This structure also housed a printing press and an office for the local newspaper. Records show that a meeting of the Court of Claims was held soon after. A committee was appointed—S.E. DeHaven, R. Rogers, Richard Waters, Moses Swim and James Hall—to oversee the construction of the new courthouse, with a budget of $10,000. The final cost was $15,780.80. M.Q. Wilson, an architect, prepared the plans. On April 19, 1875, a new courthouse opened its doors, according to the *Oldham Era* of February 19, 1937.

Hidden History of LaGrange, Kentucky

Plans drawn by architect M.O. Wilson for the 1875 Oldham County Courthouse. *Oldham County Historical Society.*

Throughout most of the twentieth century, the jail was next to the courthouse, along with the jailhouse where the jailer lived. Dennis and Bea Summit (husband and wife) have a unique situation in that both of their fathers served as jailers at the old Oldham County Jail during the 1950s and '60s. Dennis recalled experiences from times when both his father, James Summit, and his father-in-law, Clarence Moreland, served as jailer at different points and lived in the residential jailer house. Dennis described the years when he and his wife helped at the jail:

> *After Bea and I were married, we worked at the jail for Bea's father* [Clarence Moreland] *part time. Mr. Moreland was the jailer. Bea and I both worked the weekends to let Bea's father some time off. We were nineteen and twenty years old back then; we were responsible for locking people up and taking care of them. Of course, Bea grew up in the jail. Her dad was the jailer during her childhood. The living quarters for the jail were in front, had a breezeway, there on the courthouse yard.*
>
> *In between time, I worked at Anaconda for a short time, and that was a terrible place to work for me. The chemicals were so bad I got copper poisoning and had to quit. I lost all the hair off my body; it was not good. So I left and I went to work for Dad in 1978 as his deputy jailer.*
>
> *As jailer, we did everything at the jail and courthouse back then. We cooked, we cleaned the courthouse, we waited on court, took the judge water and all that. I worked twelve hours a day and every other weekend for $12,500 a year. The jail was a dungeon then. It was made from that old rock that is now over at the history center (part of it is a fountain). They said they moved that jail from Westport (when it was a county seat) and*

said it was a holding jail for slaves. When the riverboats came in, they said they brought slaves in and sold them at the courthouse there. There were four holding cells.

When people stayed in our jail, they gained weight. We all cooked at the jail—me, Bea and Bea's mom and dad. We fixed biscuits, gravy, toast, bacon, fried eggs, chili on Saturdays with peanut butter sandwiches, ice cream sandwiches, we had a grill outside, and we grilled hamburgers and chili dogs with everything. Everyone loved our chili so much; all the cops in the county came in too to eat chili on Saturdays. The cops would come in at night and eat! Then they changed the regs and jailers did not have to live near the jails.

Most of the time, everything was pretty safe, but when we kept one man (who was convicted of murder of a local person), we received death threats. People were going to come in and kill him. I had nightmares when we kept him; he was an evil man.

Nancy Timmons grew up in LaGrange, close to the courthouse, and spent many of her childhood years playing on the courthouse square with her friend, who was the jailer's daughter during the 1930s:

We roller skated and played tag at the courthouse lawn. There was a cannon there from World War I, I think, and they took it for World War II for scrap metal. It broke my heart; I sat on that cannon every day! Mr. Ransdell was the jailer and lived there at the courthouse. One of his daughters, Geneva, was a very close friend. On New Year's Eve, we got to ring the circular fire bell at twelve o'clock. Mr. Ransdell was very particular about his grass on the courthouse. Sometimes Geneva and I helped with the food and washed dishes for the inmates. Mr. Ransdell (who was a widower) had eight or nine children who lived there. I think they all helped take care of the jail. We would play all over the courtyard and jail area. I remember going into the courthouse and just running up and down the courthouse stairs and halls (until someone would tell me to leave!).

Charlie Prather remembered the Depression years, when people gathered to get their Christmas turkey on the courthouse lawn:

When we were in LaGrange, the big thing was to come to the courthouse at Christmas. They would have Santie Claus there and fly live turkeys off the balcony of the courthouse. They would let them fly down to the

Oldham County Boys and Girls Calf Club in front of the Oldham County Courthouse, circa 1930s. *Oldham County Historical Society.*

crowd, and whoever caught one got to keep it. I don't remember how many they would let fly down, but there was a big fight one time over a turkey, and they quit doing it. Santie Claus would give you a bag of candy, which was big back then because it was during the Depression, and you didn't get much back then.

Before Fiscal Court moved to the building on First and Jefferson, it was in the courthouse building along with the magistrates and county judge's office. Wendell Moore served both as a magistrate and later was elected Oldham County judge. He spoke about those years of growth as Interstate 71 opened and how that changed Oldham County:

It was 1966, and I was appointed to fill out the term of my uncle Raymond Moore. He resigned to go to work for the state. Then I ran for the office, and I was there two terms and then decided to run for judge. Judge Hall decided to retire. I ran in 1973 and took office in 1974. I held that office until 1994, when I retired. [In the early years as judge, Moore had judicial duties, which is not required of the county judges today.] I had Quarterly Court, I had Juvenile Court and we had Traffic Court every Saturday morning. At that time, when I first got involved as a magistrate, we had judicial duties as a magistrate, as a justice of the peace. Living on Highway 42, the officers over there at the time, the state police, Kentucky didn't have reciprocity with the other states. In other words, if you got picked up with a traffic violation and they let you go and you were from Ohio or Michigan or something like that, if you didn't pay your fine, nothing happened, nothing went against your record unless you happened to come back to Kentucky. So, what the officers would do, I would have Traffic Court at home as a magistrate. If they wanted to let them go and just get the ticket, they would bring them in, and you would have court then. It might be midnight. It might be one o'clock in the morning. And they didn't want to come all the way over to Judge Hall, drive all the way over here from 42, so there were three of us magistrates that lived over here on 42. Joe Nay was one and I was one, and the other was Harry Nelson.

Well, when I first took office [as county judge], there wasn't that much to do [regarding county management]. As the county began to grow, we needed a road department, we needed a parks department, we needed senior citizens programs, we needed a police department. Because at that time we just had a sheriff's department, and they didn't get enough money to have that many people. So in 1978, we formed a county police department. We started out with three officers. Then we worked with the state in getting land from the reformatory to have a county park. Then we got us a road department and started getting equipment in. But we did it as we got the money. Most of the magistrates back then, they also came up during hard times, and they sort of believed that you don't buy unless you had the money. It was pretty much how we had to do back then. There were 14,500 in Oldham County when I took office in 1974.

The salary was set by the state; $12,000 was my annual salary. That was the maximum. That was derived from the fee office. That had to come out of the fees from Quarterly Court and Traffic Court. A certain fee went to the county and a certain fee went to the state. Our salary was paid from that. I supplemented my salary with a little bit of farm work.

The courthouse has been the site of many countywide events, such as Jones Downey Day, which honored Captain Luther C. Jones and Corporal Earl Downey for their Korean War service; Governor's Day; Light-Up LaGrange, which began back in the 1950s; and Oldham County Day, sponsored by Project Guild, which began in 1971 and is still an annual event.

Governor's Day on the courthouse lawn, circa 1962. *Left to right*: Attorney and later Oldham County judge George Williamson, Governor Bert Combs and local insurance owner L.D. Cassady. *Oldham County Historical Society.*

Governor's Day was an event sponsored by the Kentucky Chamber of Commerce that escorted the Kentucky governor on a tour of small towns. The LaGrange Oldham County Chamber of Commerce hosted this event on the courthouse lawn on September 27, 1962. Merchants planned a special street sale, prizes were given away throughout the day and the Oldham County High School Band furnished the music under Guy Ashmore. Burgoo by the bucketful sold for twenty-five cents per serving. Governor Bert Combs and Colonel Harlan Sanders (of KFC fame) were special guests. Governor Combs appointed local native L.D. Cassady as the Kentucky insurance commissioner during the event.

Jean Kay Radcliffe remembered that day well because her husband, Dick Radcliffe, was one of the people in charge of the event, and he asked Jean to plan the menu. Long tables were set up on the courthouse lawn, and several hundred people attended the lunch. Jean recalled the event:

> *Rotary decided to host Governor's Day at the courthouse lawn, so Dick suggested they have burgoo, and most of the men had never had burgoo.*

Dick said, "Oh, well, I will have Jean make you some and bring some at the next meeting and see if you want it or not." I really worked that whole week! I got the rabbit, and I got the whole nine yards and got my grandmother's old recipe. They tasted it and liked it, so they decided to have it. The man at the reformatory, they had a garden and all, he had some men there that made the soup using my recipe, and it was real good and they served it.

Harry Booker remembered Saturday nights in LaGrange on the courthouse lawn in the 1940s and '50s: "LaGrange was a booming town on Saturday. There was a bandstand on the corner of the courthouse, and there was a band that would come up from the penitentiary farm and play in the afternoons on the weekend."

Beverly McCombs worked at the courthouse during the 1970s and had some funny stories to share:

I had a baby, Jaime, and then I went to work for Laura Hargrove, the circuit court clerk. She said to me, "Okay, here is the deal: go home, wean the baby (because I was breastfeeding), register Democrat and you got a job!" I was with here for eight and a half years. I started with driver's licenses. The only person that ever tipped me when I was doing licenses was Dinwiddie Lampton, and I had to explain to him, I can't take tips. And from there, I took a position as deputy clerk in district court. That was back when every ticket written or arrest made, you did it all by typewriter. I loved that job. The white folders were traffic, and the brown folders were misdemeanors. I enjoyed talking to all the attorneys. I learned about all the statutes, the numbers and prided myself in knowing what the numbers were by [statute]. Dennis Fritz was the district court judge and started the first day that I started. He was the best, and the circuit court judge was George Williamson. I did on occasion was able to back up the recorder and run the tape when court was in session; didn't do that all the time. When Judge Fritz became circuit court judge, I did a trial with him. I remember there was a bad murder and Judge Fritz saying, "Don't even look at them (the murderers) when they walk through." I also was exposed to child abuse cases, things like that.

Once there was a guy in the back of the courtroom, I think from the jail, awaiting a hearing, and was in that room alone. I was sitting at my desk, and all of a sudden, something crashes through the ceiling. This inmate had gotten up through the ceiling in the holdover room and went up and over through the removable tiles. He was trying to break out! He comes right down beside me. He was stunned, looks at us and then jumps over the counter. I started to grab him, and someone else grabbed me and said, "Whoa, come back Beverly!" I don't know what the heck I thought I was doing!

In 1990, the one-hundred-year-old jail on the courthouse lawn was torn down and replaced by a seventy-one-bed regional jail. Some of the hand-cut stones from the old jail have been repurposed for a fountain on the Oldham County History Center campus. The jail was designed to complement the classic Revival and Italianate architecture of the courthouse, and special detail was made to match the brick. During that same year, Oldham County Fiscal Court, which was meeting in the old courthouse, purchased the Citizen's Fidelity Bank on the corner of Jefferson and First Streets to renovate and moved into the old bank building. The 1875 courthouse was renovated to house District and Circuit Courts while maintaining its historic presence in LaGrange. A three-story addition was added to the rear of the building, and the building was expanded from nine thousand square feet to twenty-three thousand square feet. The project was completed in 1995 at a cost of $2.5 million.

Currently, the courthouse is undergoing another massive renovation that is to be completed in 2024. The 1875 courthouse structure is being included in a plan that will add two major wings on the east and west sides of the building, spanning to First and Second Streets. The 1990 jail was demolished in 2016, and a $23 million detention center was built on Highway 146 at Buckner and opened in January 2018.

Part V

SPECIAL PLACES

HENDRON'S GROCERY STORE

Hendron's Grocery Store was the only place open on Sundays where you could get that loaf of bread and milk until Interstate 71 opened in 1969. There were many times we stopped at Hendron's on the way home from church. Candy was displayed behind large glass cases—my favorite being sour apple bubble gum—and there were night crawlers in the cooler at the back of the store essential for a Sunday afternoon of fishing. I remember a pot-bellied stove, and they had baloney by the slice and some canned goods on the shelves behind the counters. The store sat on the boundary between Black and white neighborhoods near First and Madison Streets. Mrs. Hendron, "Toots," sat behind the counter. Her daughter Janie and I grew up together. I never saw Mr. Hendron much, but I knew he was somewhere in the back. I got to interview Herbie, Janie's older brother, for our Living Treasures Program. The following is part of Herbie's story about growing up at the grocery store.

> *Dad had a chance to buy a mom-and-pop grocery store in LaGrange at 305 North First. The grocery was near the Black section of town, and that was who most of our clients were. We lived in a house there beside the store. People who lived around us were Flora Richie, Calvin, Charlie Winburn (he trained bird dogs and stuff).... There was the First Baptist Church right across the street from the store. I would sit in front of the store*

on Sundays, and you could hear folks singing there two blocks away. There was singing, belting out tunes, and lots of preaching—amen to this, amen to that. It was really nice.

I played with a lot of Black kids; we hung out and didn't have any trouble. Schools were segregated, and I was almost in high school when integration took place. I played baseball at the colored school almost every day (which was down the street) or we played in the field between Flora Ritchie's house and our store. Clayton Renaker owned that field, and when he wasn't raising tobacco, we would play in the field. A bunch of us would get together and go fishing down there at the city lake (Mac's Lake today). Some of the kids I hung out with were Bob Allen (Rob), Larry Parrot, Billy and John Anderson. Billy went on to become a Golden Glove champion in Louisville boxing until he broke his hand. The boxing matches were on TV every Saturday night, and we would watch Billy. He came up visiting me about three months ago, and that was the first time I had seen him in thirty-four years or more. I was throwing baseball with the grandkids, and he said, "Good Lord, last time I saw you, you were playing baseball, and you are still playing baseball!"

In the summer, me and my friends would sit out in front of the store on the hot days and get watermelon and eat it all afternoon, or Mother would come out and give us ice cream and stuff. Everybody came to each other's house; it was a good time. My mother was a good cook, too. She could cook fried chicken and fried fish. I know one time, me and George Ritchie decided to skip playing ball one night and go fishing. That is the only time in my life I missed a ballgame. We caught 150 some odd fish that day. We went home and cleaned about 50 or 60 of those things, and my mom started frying them, and she fried a big plate of hot water cornbread. We sat there and ate until we about passed out. Then we went back out and fished some more. One day, we went to Mac Lake, and me and George climbed over a barbed-wire fence. I saw the biggest black snake I had ever seen. I saw that snake, turned around, jumped over the barbed-wire fence!

The grocery store was wood frame and had siding on the front. Inside, there was wood paneling and a concrete floor, and on one side Mom had all her kitchen so she could cook and tend the store. Mostly there were counters on each side. We sold bread, candy, ice cream and there was a place in the back where we sold sliced meats. Wally Nay (the county sheriff) would come and would slice his own meat. Dad would just tell Wally, "You know what you want," and Wally would slice his own meat, steaks and everything, and pay my dad. People were a lot closer than it is now.

At the candy counter, you could get Milky Ways, and all kinds of gum drops and chewing gum were popular. The little kids liked "pickled pigs' feet"; we got them from Fisher and sold them for a quarter a piece. When I got out of the service, people told me I should take the grocery over, but I looked at all the changes that were happening with larger stores moving in town and decided I didn't want it.

My parents were very trustworthy and honest and would do anything for anybody. I remember, when Dad worked for the fuel company, people would call him for fuel, and we would deliver at all times of day and night. People would call at three in the morning, and he would get up and go. He had to go downtown Louisville, off River Road, to get the fuel. Sometimes I went with him. Mom was one of those people that didn't want to tell you anything about her business, but she wanted to know what was going on. She was very friendly to everyone, but she had a temper too. We all got along well in the neighborhood; if you needed something, people would help you.

THE TAYLOR ADDITION: WEST JEFFERSON STREET

The late nineteenth- and early twentieth-century homes along Jefferson Street were known as the Taylor Addition. They were once part of the Taylor-Willett farm. The former site of the Taylor-Willet home is now the Radcliffe Funeral Home.

The following comes from an *Oldham Era* column written by Reuben "Bookie" Thorton Taylor (1891–1967), who gave a history of the Taylor-Willett home, built by his great-great-uncle William Berry Taylor. Bookie served on an ambulance and in the field artillery and at the American Embassy during World War I. He later became a well-known scholar and folk singer.

The Radcliffe Funeral Home stands on the former site of the William Berry Taylor house, built around 1800. It started as a log cabin and was added onto until it reached the size of fourteen rooms. It had huge outsized chimneys at the four corners of the house and porches on three sides, the north side having an "L" with what was known as the "back dining room" and a kitchen. Across a bricked area there was a dairy and well. A flagged walk extended for the entire block to what, after the 1850s was called "Railroad Street." Another flagged walk, lined with cherry trees, extended east to what is Third Street.

The property was left to Elizabeth (Taylor) Willett, one of William Berry Taylor's daughters. (Elizabeth's husband was Dr. John Willett, who was from Shelbyville. They had no children.) She was better known as Cousin Betsy, and she left this property, after her death to her niece, Bettie Mallory—a granddaughter of one of the Mallory Family who gave the Mallory-Taylor Hospital to LaGrange.

It was from her that my grandfather, Ruben Thornton Taylor (1820–1891), bought the old house and the land, which later was known as Taylor Addition. My father, P.D. Taylor (1861–1940) built the first house on an extension of Jefferson Street—the first of many houses built on lots sold to keep the family going. It wasn't exactly a goldmine, but it didn't cost much to live in those days. In addition, they (my grandmother and her unmarried sons and daughters) "took in" summer boarders, as did our cousins, the Berrys at Anita Springs; and other cousins, the Clarks, just across the way, also took in summer boarders. That was a way of life for owners of big houses in the 1890's. In the 25 years following the Civil War, servants could be had for $3 a week, and having boarders was the solution to the financial problems of the owners of these large houses.

Another one of P.D.'s sons, Rowan Barclay Taylor (1893–1931), started the laundry that was located on Fourth Street that replaced the family canning operation. Around the corner at 400 Fourth Avenue (circa 1918) lived Rowan Barclay Taylor and his wife, Verna Garr Taylor. Verna (1896–1936) was the victim of a famous murder case that has resulted in numerous magazine articles and books; two of the most recent are *Dark Highway* (2016) by Ann D'Angelo and *A Black Night for the Bluegrass Belle* (2016) by Ian Punnett.

Special Places

Opposite: This home—built in the early 1800s by William Berry Taylor and later occupied by Taylor's daughter Elizabeth Taylor Willett and her husband, Dr. John Willett—was razed for McCarty Ricketts Mortuary in the 1930s. *Oldham County Historical Society*.

Above: Known as the Taylor Addition along Jefferson Street, these homes, still intact today, were once part of the Willett property. *Oldham County Historical Society*.

After Rowan's death, Verna began dating the former lieutenant governor of Kentucky, Henry Denhardt. He gave her a ring, but she didn't consider them to be engaged. On the night she decided to give him the ring back, she ended up dead; her body was found on State Road 22 with a bullet through her heart. Denhardt was brought to trial for the murder but claimed that Verna had committed suicide, distraught because he was breaking up with her.

The trial ended with a hung jury, and as he was awaiting a new trial, Denhardt was shot by two of Verna's brothers in what was called a "code of honor" killing. The brothers were acquitted of murder. Before the death of Verna, Denhardt had been questioned in the death of a woman named Patricia Wilson, who fell or was pushed down a service elevator at the Seelbach Hotel in Louisville. Her ghost, known as the "Lady in Blue," is thought to haunt the premises.

P.D. Taylor was Parker Dudley Taylor, who lived in the house at 402 Fourth Avenue (circa 1918). The house at the corner of Fourth and Madison was once owned by the famous movie director D.W. Griffith. He bought the house for his mother, who died shortly after the purchase, but he kept it in the family through the 1930s. He composed part of his autobiography while living in the house with his third wife, Evelyn Baldwin.

Other prominent LaGrange citizens who lived on Jefferson Street included Charles Davis at 309 West Jefferson. He was the pharmacist who bought McDowell Pharmacy and later sold it to Billy Head. Willie and Charles Fisher lived at 318 West Jefferson (circa 1903). Charles worked as foreman for the Louisville and Nashville Railroad. Many of the trees standing along the street are from the original planting in the early 1900s.

The McCarty and Ricketts Funeral Home

The McCarty and Ricketts Funeral Home at 311 West Main Street was built in 1936, designed by Joe Bright, a native of Eminence and graduate of the University of Pennsylvania School of Architecture. In 1948, Richard Radcliffe and his wife, Jean, became caretakers of the home, and the name was changed to the Radcliffe Funeral Home. Richard was the great-grandson of Mr. Ricketts. By 1974, the Radcliffe Funeral Home and Adkins Funeral home had merged into the Adkins-Radcliffe Funeral Home. Cecil Adkins succeeded the G.W. Peak Funeral Home on Main Street before the merger with Radcliffe. In later years, the funeral home merged into another partnership and became the Heady-Radcliffe Funeral Home and then moved into a new location in 2019.

The best example of Colonial Revival–style architecture in LaGrange and most distinctive building in the district, this two-story square plan structure was designed to house a funeral home on the first floor and a residence above. The building is framed with terra-cotta block, and the first floor has a poured concrete floor supported by railroad rails.

Lucy Radcliffe Ricketts, daughter of Richard and Jean, gave some of the history of the business:

> *Growing up in the funeral home seemed very normal to me. Mrs. Peak, who had been in the funeral home business, called my mom and told her she had a book she wanted to give me. So I went to her house, and she gave me the book titled* There's Always a Body at Our House. *It was about a little girl growing up in a funeral home, and it was just about some of the stories she wrote growing up in a funeral home. I remember thinking, "Oh, I guess this is unusual."*

Special Places

McCarty Ricketts Mortuary was later operated as the Radcliffe Funeral Home by Rickett's grandson Richard Radcliffe and his wife, Jean, through the 1990s. *Ricketts Radcliffe Collection, Oldham County Historical Society.*

We didn't have any carpet in the halls where we lived, above the funeral parlor, so you could easily hear Linda and I running up and down the hall, so Mother would put us both on top of the bed and try to entertain us during the funeral service!

Of course, there was no ambulance service, so funeral homes took that over. Stoess did one part of the county, and we did the other. If there was a wreck on Highway 42, the police would call in, and Dad would go pick them up and take them to Mallory Taylor or in Louisville, and I went on some ambulance calls with him. Highway 42 always was the road with the wrecks before the interstate opened. Dad and Fisher Hardin, who was the state police officer at the time, had all kinds of stories. One time, there were two men down in Westport who had run off the road, and Dad got to the site with Fisher Hardin, and Dad went down to get one of the men, and the other jumped in the ambulance and drove off! It seemed like the state police were often at our home.

The Frozen Food Locker

By the mid-1970s, farms began to be replaced with subdivisions in Oldham County. Up until that time, most people grew up on the family farm, where they raised much of their food, such as beef, pork, dairy, poultry and vegetables. Most farms had cisterns or wells for water and relied on coal or propane for heat, and many homes were not air conditioned. Many folks did not have freezers for food storage, so there was a local slaughterhouse where animals were killed and processed and then carried to a local meat locker.

Families rented their locker, and when they needed meat, they would visit their local meat locker and take home just what they needed for a day or two. That is exactly the way my family operated on our family farm; we went to LaGrange to get our meat from the locker. It was an important part of our food storage and continued through the mid-1960s, when freezers became cheaper and people could afford them in their homes.

The whole history of freezing food was revolutionary for the American family. Instead of relying on short-term storage of root cellars, cold-water springs, canning or salt and cured meat, food could easily be frozen and stored for months. It was also healthier and less likely to cause botulism or bacterial and fungus spoilage. The process of families freezing food began as early as 1908 by H.K. Eames from Chico, California. He offered farmers the facilities of his Chico Ice and Cold Storage Company for meat storage, including a room with a chopping block and butcher tools. The farmer had to do his own wrapping, cutting and placing meat in the locker.

In 1928, the first establishment was built for the primary purpose of renting frozen food lockers in Parsons, Kansas. In 1934, Rex Coal & Ice Co. in Creston, Iowa, was the first locker to offer processing services and storage. In the mid-1930s, builders of locker plants and locker plant equipment organized the Frozen Food Locker Manufacturers. By the late 1930s, Frozen Food Locker Manufacturers was known as Frozen Food Locker Institute (FFLI)–Supplier Group.

By the 1940s, frozen food lockers could be found across the United States, like the one in LaGrange. Cold storage locker establishments were forced to diversify their business to stay in business and began to offer more services to their customers. Chilling and aging carcasses under controlled temperature maintained the quality of the meat, as well as decreased spoilage that might occur under less-than-ideal conditions. Meat-cutting services ensured uniform thickness any way the customer requested. Wrapping services and fast-freezing technology helped maintain the quality of the finished product.

Curing and smoking services were also offered under controlled temperatures and sanitary conditions and performed by experts in the meat industry.

The following are some personal experiences at the Frozen Food Locker:

David Monroe

OK, of course I remember the Frozen Food Locker and all that stuff. My dad was on the board down there. A whole bunch of guys here in town put up about $500 apiece—Al D. Hampton, Dad, Cassadys, Oren Oakley and one or two others. They had a slaughter pen down the street. They slaughtered all this meat. You take a hog in there or a steer, they would slaughter it all out for you and charge so much, and they had a big locker back here and froze it. They would lock it all up, wrap it for you, give you the key. Then you come back and get anything you want.

Ernie Henson

In the fall of 1964, I started work at the Frozen Food Locker in LaGrange. Owen Oglesby was the manager, and Mamie Allen George was the bookkeeper. John L. Fisher ran the slaughterhouse, where the Chevron Service Station is now (across from McDonald's). All the guts and blood ran through a pipe down to the creek (that is still there today). Mr. Jesse Crockett and Mr. Charles Knight helped at the slaughterhouse. The Frozen Food Locker is where the Cassady Insurance is located today. You brought your animal to the slaughterhouse, they killed it for you, then we brought it to the Frozen Food Locker, packaged it and put it in the locker. You could come get your meat daily, or whenever you wanted. It was hard work. I had to lift sides of beef twice my weight. We took an open-bed pickup truck to the slaughterhouse. And meat was hanging in sides from a rail. You had to take a hand saw and knife and cut the hind quarter from the fore quarter, then put it in the truck, take it to the locker, use a chain hook hoist to lift it and put it in the coolers. The meat that was slaughtered was only for people who raised it, cows, hogs, sheep. Ashbourne Farms—they had the restaurant at the time—would bring five head of cattle a week to get slaughtered; the reformatory would bring ten head of cattle a week. We were a regular grocery store; we sold vegetables, bread, all that. I had two ladies that wrapped the meat for me, Marjorie Buntain and Fidelia Rogers.

Jimmy Oldson

After I got out of high school, the first job I had I worked at the Frozen Food Locker where Cassaday Insurance is now. My job was killing chickens and picking them; they had an electric chicken picker. Lawrence Till Doty and I worked there. His job was to haul chicken entrails and feathers to the reformatory incinerator. That was a dirty, filthy job, and I thought I had to do something better than that. Ware Bowman ran the Kroger Store, and I got into contact with Ware, and I worked at Kroger for a year and three months.

Bob Arvin

I can recall a little bit of slaughtering on the farm, but there was an old slaughterhouse where the Cracker Barrel is now, and the meat would be stored in the old Frozen Food Locker (where Doty Insurance is today). We would eat the liver first, then work through the rest of the meat; we would eat liver for two weeks. I like liver, but after two weeks, I was ready to eat something else. You rented space at the Frozen Food Locker to store your meat. The same people that ran the slaughterhouse ran the Frozen Food Locker.

Mallory Taylor Hospital

From January 1940 through the early 1970s, Mallory Taylor Hospital was the location of countless newborn babies, tonsillectomies and appendectomies for many of the residents of Oldham County. It was established through the estate of Oldham County native Robert Mallory, who was born in 1851 on a farm about two miles south of Ballardsville off Highway 53. The homestead was known as Oak Knoll, which was an original tract that as in the Taylor family. Mallory was the great-grandson of William Berry Taylor.

Mallory inherited his family's fortune and never married. He supported the local arts in the Louisville area and traveled extensively. Near the end of his life, he decided to leave $80,000 of his estate to establish a hospital in the Oldham County community. Before he died in 1937, he worked with a local attorney, Ballard Clarke, to set up the trust that would establish the Mallory Taylor Hospital.

The hospital, incorporated in 1938, was a model for modern medical practices at the time. The hospital was built on six acres that was the site of a former residence destroyed by fire in the 1920s. The former home had over fourteen rooms and was called Valhalla. The hospital contained living quarters for the superintendent, who resided on site.

Special Places

Robert Mallory donated $80,000 from his estate to build Mallory Taylor Hospital in LaGrange, which opened in January 1940. *Oldham County Historical Society*.

Mallory requested that portraits of the Taylor and Mallory families be displayed in the reception room of the hospital. Today, the portraits are displayed at the Oldham County History Center. The hospital had a major operating room, minor operating room, X-ray room, sterilizer room, surgeon's washroom and dark room for developing X-rays.

Patient rooms consisted of two private rooms, five semiprivate rooms, one male ward that could accommodate six patients and one female ward that could accommodate six patients. On the east side of the hospital, there were nurses' quarters with an additional room for student nurses.

The main floor was constructed with reinforced concrete of fireproof construction, and the exterior walls were made of load-bearing tile that was faced with native limestone. The roof was covered with slate-covered asphalt shingles, and the interior floors were covered with asphalt tile to reduce noise.

The hospital included a wing that was set aside for the use of any aged, indigent women who had resided in Oldham, Henry, Carroll or Shelby County; however, there was a special clause that denied treatment to African Americans unless they were kin to the Taylor or Mallory families. Africans Americans had to travel to Louisville for hospital care. Frances Walters recalled what it was like when the hospital was segregated:

We could not have our children at Mallory Taylor Hospital. You had to have them at home or go to Friendship Manor in Pewee Valley. Mallory Taylor would not have anything to do with Black people. One of my brothers (because I took care of some of my brothers too) was playing and was thrown off his bike, and he slid, and there was gravel all under his skin and in his head too. I took him up to Mallory Taylor, and they would not touch him. So we had to go to Friendship Manor.

Like most hospitals at that time, there were strictly enforced visiting hours, and children under the age of twelve were not allowed in the hospital, even if they were accompanied by an adult. Jimmy Oldson remembers when he was one of the first patients for surgery at Mallory Taylor:

In 1940, right after my birthday in March, we had been in town, and it was storming. I had an attack of appendicitis (before my leg amputation) and had an operation at Mallory Taylor, and Dr. Walsh called a surgeon, Dr. Hall, from Louisville. The hospital was new (I was the third patient), and the lights went off when they were operating on me. They didn't know how to start that Delco system up. Finally got it going and had a successful outcome.

Ruby Duncan volunteered at Mallory Taylor when she was a teenager:

During the summer between my freshman and sophomore classes [at LaGrange High School], *I worked at Mallory Taylor. I thought I would like to be a nurse and worked as a nurse's aide. Dr. Blaydes said some of us could watch him deliver a baby. He said to us, "Now if you get sick or feel faint, go sit in that corner. Don't bother me; I can't take care of you and my patient at the same time. And don't go out that door either!" The baby arrived, and we didn't get sick or faint. Then he let us watch a major surgery. He told us the same thing again. Everything went well, and the patient made it. Next, we watched him put a steel pin in someone's hip, and that did it. I never wanted to be a nurse again!*

Cindy Green worked as a nurse at Mallory Taylor Hospital during its last years of operation, when it was operated by Baptist East. In the following, she recalls her experiences as a nurse before the facility closed permanently in 1988:

The doctors out here were Dr. Norvelle, Dr. Houchin, Dr. Funke, Dr. White, Dr. Wellman, but Dr. Walsh had retired. Mallory Taylor at that time had an emergency room, hospital and nursing home, some acute care like flu or bladder infections. They didn't do surgery or delivery at that time; it was gone. They didn't tell me when I began there that there had been a robbery. I think it was Mrs. Dawson and a couple had been tied up and robbed. So, they put guards there—Steve Sparrow and Jeff Money and Ernie Powell—they moonlighted as night guards. They also worked as EMTs.

One night, I had a patient there on a cardiac monitor, and I didn't know anything about a cardiac monitor. But I knew this man was not doing well, and it was snowing out—that big snow in '78 or '79—so I called Dr. Wellman and said this man was not doing well, so I sent EMTs to go get Dr. Wellman and bring him to the hospital. So, then the ambulance pulled up quick, and I thought boy, they got Dr. Wellman real fast, but it wasn't him. They had a lady having a baby, and I said, "Not in here she's not." And I started praying—all those prayers I had learned. They said to come out to check her, so I did, and I said, "Oh, sweet Jesus." She was crowning, so I said bring her in....I caught the baby. The woman is thanking me, and then Dr. Wellman came in and said, "What's going on?" and I said, "We are having a baby." So, he cut the cord and we cleaned up, and Dr. Wellman said, "How is the man?" And I said, "He is probably dead; I have been delivering the baby!" That was the last baby born at Mallory Taylor.

Mallory Taylor has been completely razed, but it was located on the corner of Jefferson Street and Dawkins School Road.

The Belle of LaGrange

In July 1969, LaGrange changed dramatically. Interstate Highway 71 opened, providing a new route from Louisville to Cincinnati, replacing U.S. Highway 42, which in the mid-1960s was dubbed one of the ten most dangerous highways in the United States. There is no doubt change was necessary because U.S. 42 had become a huge traffic jam, with dangerous curves and small-town thoroughfares that made travel long, difficult and burdensome for the traveler.

The Belle of LaGrange was one of the first fast-food restaurants in the area after Interstate 71 opened in 1969. *Oldham County Historical Society.*

Dubbed as the Derby Highway, the loss of the Highway 42 corridor resulted in the loss of mom-and-pop restaurants and small car motels for towns like Bedford, Ghent, Carrollton and Warsaw that depended on the traffic. In LaGrange, business began to develop along the interstate corridor. Small grocery stores, restaurants and retail businesses disappeared along Main Street.

The first fast-food restaurant in LaGrange that I remember was the Belle of LaGrange, which opened in the first week in December 1970. The owners were Charlie and Mary (Marjorie) Ransdell of Bedford. The restaurant itself was a tourist attraction, built like a paddle wheeler, reflecting the steamboat history of the region and the Ohio River.

The restaurant dished up fast food fare such as cheeseburgers, French fries and fried fish sandwiches. Frances Timberlake Walters recalled her time working at the Belle of LaGrange:

I first started cooking for the Belle of LaGrange sometimes in the '70s. I loved that place; I would have owned that place if I could. It was built like a big ship. There was an upstairs and downstairs. The Ransdells owned it. They made their own chicken cookers. We made our own strawberry pies. We had to cap them, cut them and make up a big kettle of strawberry glaze. We made the glaze the night before and put the glaze in the walk-in cooler so it would cool overnight. Majorie and my daughter Victoria worked with her in the afternoon at the Belle. One day, Majorie came in after me, and she forgot about the glaze. She backed out the door and put her foot down in the kettle of hot glaze. She had blisters everywhere. We bought the crust for the pie, put the strawberries and glaze in then topped the pie with Cool Whip. We had fried biscuits, and we bought Icelandic cod and made our own special seasoned meal to dip them in. We made our own salad, hand-cut slaw and onion rings. We used a mayonnaise dressing on the slaw. They closed the Belle in 1978; they went bankrupt. It was such a beautiful place. It was my heart.

Anita Springs and the Royal Inn

Shortly after the Revolutionary War, Lieutenant John Russell of Henrico, Virginia, received a sizable land grant for his services to the United States. Receiving nearly three thousand acres of land in what was to later become Oldham County, Russell moved his wife, Hannah, and their twelve children to the new frontier. Russell discovered his property contained one prominent and important feature: five natural limestone springs. The prominent spring was located half a mile from the center of downtown LaGrange. These natural limestone springs became very popular vacation spots, attracting families from throughout the country who would bring their families to Kentucky for extended visits. While some would come for the "curative powers" of the clear spring waters, others came merely for a season of socializing. These springs also became popular for mixing drinks such as bourbon and branch.

In 1877, Dr. James Thornley Berry and his wife, Anita, bought two hundred acres of the property that was formerly owned by Lieutenant John Russell that contained the prominent spring. Berry named the property Anita Springs after his wife and began bottling the mineral spring water. In 1894, he started shipping jugs of the water to Louisville by the L&N Railroad, which passed through the Anita Springs property and stopped at the gate.

By 1903, demands for Dr. Berry's mineral water had increased so that he felt obliged to start the Anita Water Company. He located his office at 721 South Second Street in Louisville. Within a matter of months after establishing his business, ill health forced him to turn operations over to Robert Brooke, husband of Berry's daughter, Anita Anderson Berry Brooke.

With Dr. Berry's death in 1905, Brook made several changes in the company. He moved the office to 210 Pearl Street in Louisville and constructed a bottling plant at that location. The new site took advantage of the interurban electric railway, whose tracks ran parallel to the L&N Railroad on the Anita Springs property. With the convenience of a platform built by the interurban on Anita Springs property, workmen could transport large barrels of water from the spring to the on-site loading facility. From there, the cargo of water would travel to the plant entrance in Louisville. The Berry family continued to run Anita Water Company until 1918, when it was sold.

The Royal Magnusson Inn was using the natural spring water in the same vicinity. The inn was built around the railroad, interurban and car traffic. It survived for about twenty years until it burned down sometime in the early 1920s.

The Public Spring

The Public Spring, on the corner of Second and Washington, is on a parcel of land donated by William Berry Taylor to establish the city of LaGrange. Until a city water system came into being in 1930, the spring was a source of water to nearby farms and homes. Even when other springs or creeks dried up in the summer months, the Public Spring always ran. People often drove their horse and buggy to the spring when they visited LaGrange. Diane Booker remembered how important the spring once was:

> *I live in the same place on Second Street today where I grew up* [across from the old Kynett Methodist Church]. *We tore down the old house I lived in as a child and rebuilt the one we live in now. There was all farmland around us back then. We had a horse barn behind us and a pig farm. There was the Public Spring, which is still there today and running, and that is where we got our water. People would come and get their water; they would bring barrels and take it to their farms. That is where we got our water before there was running water in LaGrange until the oil from Hammonds, a car garage up on the hill from the spring, leaked their oil from the car garage. The water became polluted, so people had to stop drinking the water.*

Part VI
Special Homes

William Todd Barbour House: 203 East Washington Street

The William Todd Barbour home may date as early as 1830 and is probably the oldest remaining building in the LaGrange historic district and the only Federal-style brick home that remains. It was built for William Todd Barbour (1791–1846), whose first wife, Mary Berry Taylor (1800–1833), was the daughter of William Berry Taylor. William Barbour remarried in 1834 to Eleanor Madison Taylor (1802–1883), who was a niece of William Berry Taylor. Barbour was also a surveyor and laid out the plan for LaGrange. In 1846, the home became a girls' dormitory for Funk Seminary, which became the Kentucky Masonic College. For many years after the school closed, it was a multifamily dwelling. It has been totally renovated and restored to its original beauty primarily by one of its owners, Linda Foster.

Linda was a good friend of mine, and I interviewed her for an article for the *Courier-Journal* when I was a featured columnist. Through the interview, she related the following:

> *I purchased the house in 1993 from Kate Travis, widow of Joe Travis, who renovated the house beginning in the late 1980s. The home was in complete disrepair until the Travises renovated the home. Several years after his death, Kate reluctantly decided to sell the house. The only item left in the house that was a personal effect of the Travises was a large mirror they had purchased in an auction from the Red Cross building in Louisville. I*

William T. Barbour was a surveyor and son-in-law of William Berry Taylor. His home is one of the oldest brick structures in LaGrange and served as a girls' dormitory for the Kentucky Masonic College. *Author's collection.*

kept the mirror hanging in the foyer of the house, and it became a focal point for ghost stories.

I opened a retail store around 1995, Christmas in Kentucky, on the first floor of the home and lived on the second floor. From that point, ghostly experiences became ordinary instead of extraordinary. I had customers say they would look in the window and then quickly look away because they said it made them feel uncomfortable.

One day, a gentleman looked at the mirror, felt strangely and told me he saw an image of a woman. When I looked into the mirror, I saw something I had never seen before: an image of a Victorian woman—quite possibly a nurse. Others have reported seeing it as well.

The most significant encounter for me occurred upstairs. One night—in the middle of the night—I awoke abruptly. I felt the sensation of someone holding my hand. It felt like a thin, frail person holding on very tightly. I sat up in bed, placed my other hand on top of the hand being "held" and began rubbing my hand but couldn't see anything. The sensation continued for quite a while.

Another time, I was getting something out of my storage closet, which is located under the front stairs. When I opened the door, there was an extremely strong odor of ammonia. It was overpowering, causing me to step back. I was familiar with the odor because of a childhood problem with fainting, and ammonia smelling salts were used to revive me. I quickly shut the closet door, and when I went back later to check, the smell was completely gone. Possibly, I thought, the nurse was administering ammonia to me, trying to communicate with me that she was in the house.

We believe the ghost of the nurse came with the mirror to the house, and she is making sure everyone here is well cared for. We have no idea how many people have seen the nurse over the years, but the owner does know that many people have glanced strangely at the mirror, some doing a double-take. I have had others come into the store and say they have seen several young girls standing at the top of the steps. Several others have mentioned seeing a cat walk through the store. One time, a woman who was shopping in the house asked me if I had experienced any ghosts in the house. She said she was very sensitive and there were many ghosts here, but they are friendly and very caring.

Linda opened her house to the Main Street Ghost Tours, and over the years, the mirror in the foyer seemed to change, adding images of soldiers on horses, hills and trees and various other scenes. Unfortunately, Linda died in 2015, and the home was sold. The current owners are maintaining its historic presence and have plans for the house in the near future. In my interview with Linda, she said that when she died, she planned to come back and be a ghost in the house and haunt all its future visitors!

Rob Morris House: 110 East Washington Street

At the intersection of Washington and Walnut Streets, there are pre–Civil War buildings, still extant, one of which was the home of Dr. Rob Morris (1818–1888). As Morris came "into the light," he donned his Masonic apron and carried the ideals of Freemasonry through a despairing time of American history. His voluminous writing on Freemasonry and his ability to pen poems that celebrated occasions or honored the deceased earned him the title of poet laureate of Freemasonry in the nineteenth century.

In addition to his Masonic poetry, Morris created the Order of the Eastern Star, which included women in the Masonic Order. At the time

ROB MORRIS HOME, LaGrange, Ky.

Dr. Rob Morris house. Morris was the nineteenth-century poet laureate of Freemasonry and founder of the Order of the Eastern Star. *Oldham County Historical Society.*

Morris created the Eastern Star degrees, the first women's rights convention was being held at the Wesleyan Chapel in Seneca Falls, New York, on July 19, 1848. The Declaration of Sentiments issued at the convention declared that even though the Constitution of the United States declared that all are equal, there was a "long train of abuses and usurpations" of "patient sufferances of the women under this government." The time was ripe for the women's movement.

Morris became a permanent resident in LaGrange when he came in 1860 to teach at the Kentucky Masonic College. By the time he arrived in LaGrange, he had established enough connections to earn the title of LLD conferred by the Kentucky Masonic College and thence forward referred to himself as Dr. Rob Morris.

The Morrises moved into a home on Second Street, but it burned down, so they purchased their permanent home on Washington Street from the Taliferro family. This home became the permanent residence for Rob and Charlotte Morris, their seven children and their beloved dog, Leo, a large shepherd mix that accompanied Morris on his walks through town.

Special Homes

The outbreak of the Civil War affected everyone and every institution in the South. Kentucky Masonic College was no different. Enrollment quickly receded, and mounting deficits became problematic. Morris had taken over leadership of the college. He also continued his efforts to strengthen the conservators' movement, but both began to weaken as the Civil War began to take its toll.

By the mid-1860s, Morris had turned his attention to the fulfillment of his longtime dream to visit the Holy Land. In 1866, Morris gave his blessing and endorsement to his friend Robert Macoy to take over the organization of the Eastern Star so he could raise funds for his trip to the Holy Land. Morris continued his massive correspondences, lectures and writings. He also loved the science of numismatics and published in a LaGrange newspaper on the subject.

By the time Morris died, he had traveled to three continents, visited more than three thousand lodges and penned over seventy volumes of work that included close to four hundred poems. The largest volume of poems by Morris, *The Poetry of Freemasonry*, was published in 1884, the same year that Morris was crowned poet laureate.

Morris remained in fairly good health until six weeks before his death on July 31, 1888. He was interred at the Valley of Rest Cemetery in LaGrange. His grave marker is a tall obelisk that stands out and is easily found. His wife is buried with him, and some family members are buried there along with the Mounts family.

LaGrange native Marjorie Morgan has been an active member of the Rob Morris Chapter OES and overseen the care of the Rob Morris Historic Home. She explained how the home today is an important part of the Masonic organization:

> *I got active in Eastern Star when the boys were almost grown. David [Morgan, my husband] became a trustee for the Rob Morris home in 1967, and that has been our prime interest in Eastern Star because of the Rob Morris home. Ruby Jesse's parents were curators when I was growing up, and I played with Ruby when we were little before I knew anything about Rob Morris.*
>
> *Every year, we have a pilgrimage at the Rob Morris home. He was born on August 31 and died on July 31, so the third Sunday of August every year, we have a program that honors Rob Morris that brings some point of his life we talk about. Then we go down to his memorial. He was a Masonic writer and came to LaGrange as a teacher at the Funk Seminary*

in 1860. He was very well read, educated up East. He was primarily known in the Masonic circles and was a good teacher, lecturer and true, more fluent in Masonic teachings, but knew a lot about a lot of things. He was a coin collector, did a lot of Masonic journals, was a publisher in Louisville. We usually have a few hundred people come and have had as many as seven hundred come.

Rob Morris was one of the founders of the LaGrange Presbyterian Church, which he called "dear to his heart," where he recited his poetry and played hymns that he composed. The church, at 207 West Jefferson, now serves as the Rob Morris Chapel Education Building on the Oldham County History Center campus. In 2015, the Grand Chapter of Kentucky dedicated a plaque on the church façade to the memory of Rob Morris.

Buddy Pepper House: 109 Walnut Street

It is hard to miss the Buddy Pepper childhood home in LaGrange. A large wooden tree sculpture titled *The Watchman* overshadows the small shotgun house that dates to the 1840s. This original structure was part of the William Barbour home across the street and could possibly have been slave quarters. The home, which has been through several remodels, has a marker to identify the homeplace of this iconic 1940s/1950s pop musician and childhood actor.

Buddy Pepper (1922–1993, born in LaGrange as Jack Starkey) was a composer, pianist and child star during the pre- and postwar era of World War II. His most popular hit, "Vaya Con Dias," is still a recognizable pop tune that has been recorded by over two hundred artists. Buddy began playing the piano by ear and singing as a child. He made a concert debut at age eleven as a piano soloist with the Steedman Symphony in Louisville. He appeared on WHAS radio in the 1930s, followed by a succession of local appearances that included Louisville's Loew's Theatre and the Kentucky State Fair. He moved to Louisville by his teens and began vaudeville sets on stage. "I remember an all-night blockbuster benefit show at the Rialto, when I appeared on the bill with Baby Rose Marie, a big child star then."

By the age of fourteen, he got a big break when he auditioned for a vaudeville act for Jack Pepper (Ginger Rogers's first husband) and appeared in Pepper's vaudeville act posing as Jack Pepper's little brother, along with

Florence Krauss as Pepper's little sister. From then on, Starkey changed his name to Buddy Pepper and fulfilled his desire to go to Hollywood and perform. This move led to his first movie contract for *That Certain Age*, a 1938 movie starring Deanna Durbin. His best-known performances were in *Small Town Deb* and *Golden Hoofs* opposite leading lady Jane Withers. He was also featured in Walt Disney's *Reluctant Dragon*, *Seventeen*, *Men of Boys Town* and the "Henry Aldrich" series. Although Pepper enjoyed being an actor, his greatest love was music, and he began writing movie scores and being an accompanist and arranger for such well-known performers as Judy Garland, Margaret Whiting, Lisa Kirk and Marlene Dietrich.

Child film star and pop songwriter Buddy Pepper lived at 109 South Walnut across from the Barbour house. *Oldham County Historical Society*.

In fact, Buddy and Judy Garland became lifelong friends, and Pepper gave Garland and her first husband, Dave Rose, credit for encouraging his career path toward composing songs. Pepper even accompanied Garland in her debut at London's Palladium Theatre in 1951. Pepper recalls the opening at the Palladium in an article he wrote:

> *Her performance went smoothly until she finished the fourth number. At this time, we were both supposed to exit. Suddenly the audience fell silent and looking toward the mike, I saw no Judy. However, right behind it, there was our girl—sitting flat on her you-know-what, stage center. I let out a howl, as she did, walked over to her and helped her to her feet. The audience started yelling and laughing with us, with which Judy threw her arms around me, gave me a big smack.*
>
> *It wasn't until Judy started to sing her final number, "Over the Rainbow," that I finally really realized what happened. We were on at the Palladium. A baby spot was on Judy—and she'd done it. They started to roar before she'd even sung the last lyric—and as the curtains folded in on the final words: "Why, oh why, can't I?" it was bedlam.*
>
> *We were a bit bewildered by some of the newspaper reviews. They lauded Judy's performance, yet they commented on her weight, her gown, her vocal volume, and naturally, all mentioned her fall. But we knew, above all, she'd been a hit. By noon that day, her four weeks' engagement was sold out.*

During World War II, Pepper was assigned to the Special Services Section of the U.S. Army. He traveled on a twelve-thousand-mile circuit that included Alaska, performing in various army shows for servicemen and women.

Pepper signed contracts over the years with Universal Studios, Famous Music Company and Paramount Pictures Corporation. He wrote songs for feature films including "When Johnny Comes Marching Home," "Top Man," "Chip Off the Old Block," "Senorita from the West," "This Is the Life," "Sing a Jingle," "Mister Big," "The Hucksters," "The Winning Team," "Portrait in Black" and, probably the most well-known of his musical scores, "Pillow Talk," produced by Martin Melcheris, starring Doris Day and Rock Hudson.

Individual hits written by Pepper included "Don't Tell Me," "How You've Gone and Hurt My Southern Pride," "Nobody but You," "Sorry," "That's the Way He Does It," "Kitten with My Mittens Laced," "The Spirit Is in Me," "Niagara," "Serenade," "Boogie Woogie Sandman," "Samba Sue," "All to Myself," "You Look Good to Me," "Chant of the Tom Tom," "Manhattan Isle," "Madame Mozelle," "God Bless Us Everyone," "I Just Kissed My Nose Goodnight," "Oldham County Line," "It's Lonely," "Hup Two Three Four Blues" and "This Must Be a Dream."

Dr. Hubert Blaydes House and Hospital

Dr. Hubert Blaydes (1876–1946) and his wife, Susie, lived in a beautiful two-story frame home with a large wraparound porch by the railroad tracks in LaGrange. The home served as Dr. Blayde's office as well as a small hospital for his patients who required surgery. He was a World War I veteran.

He became a national figure when he and another LaGrange doctor, J.T. Walsh, conducted forensic experiments in the widely publicized Verna Garr Taylor murder case. Taylor was shot and killed, supposedly by her fiancé, General Denhardt. Blaydes testified in the murder trial about the hole made by the fatal bullet that entered the chest under Taylor's left breast. The unusual aspect for the testimony was that Walsh, along with Drs. Blaydes and Miller, used a pig carcass to demonstrate bullet wounds and their effect on the skin at close range. Pieces of slip undergarment from Taylor's clothing were laid on each of the test sites of the pig from a fired bullet at three, six, nine and eighteen inches. The point of the demonstration was to show that Taylor could not have committed suicide.

The evidence remained inconclusive after several sustained objections from the defense counsel.

The following are stories about Dr. Blaydes from some of his patients:

J.W. Hall

I got scarlet fever when I was fourteen, and I was quarantined. I got a heart murmur from it. I was out of school for a month. Dr. Alexander and Dr. Walsh were the two doctors around. Dr. Alexander was in Crestwood, and Dr. Walsh was in LaGrange. Now, I knew Dr. Blaydes, but he had pretty much stopped practicing when I was growing up. He had that big house, which used to be where the parking lot and skateboard park is today, across from the fire station. He used to operate on people, there in his home, on the kitchen table. My grandmother had sugar diabetes, and she had to have her toe taken off. So Doc Blaydes said, "Get up there on the table, Mrs. Steele, I need to take that toe off." He cut that toe right off! He might have given her a shot to help numb it. They used pot ash back then, to soak her toe in, so it wouldn't get infected.

Ruby Duncan

I had a pain in my right side, so I made it to Dr. Blaydes's office. He said, "Missy, I'm going to send you down to Pewee Valley and get a blood count." I went to the Pewee Valley hospital for that and returned to Dr. Blaydes with the results. Dr. Blaydes said, "Well, you have appendicitis." He removed my appendix and made me stay in the hospital two weeks. That surgery was at Mallory Taylor Hospital about 1943.

Nancy Oglesby

There were very few cars in LaGrange; mainly we just got around on foot. Dr. Blaydes had a car. He delivered me at home. Mother fell down the steps just two weeks before I was born, and he came to see her. He believed he should stay, so he stayed at our house and delivered me the next morning.

Dr. Blaydes's house was across from the interurban station and DeHaven Baptist Church (down by the history center today, across the tracks). It was a big white two-story house, and the Brents lived there years later. Dr. Blaydes used his house as a hospital, and my mother was operated on there. They took me there to see her. They had a little rocking chair. I was about two, and they said I sat there and rocked by her bed. The hospital was upstairs, and his office was downstairs, and he and his wife lived in back of the house. I think it was that way for years!

David Wark Griffith House: 206 Fourth Avenue

Dubbed "One of the Most Influential People in the Twentieth Century" by the *Saturday Evening Post*, D.W. Griffith (1875–1948) was called the "Father of Modern Film," producing four hundred films during his career. He created such filmmaking techniques as the fadeout, flashback, diffused lighting, moving cameras and high-angle photography.

When D.W. Griffith (1875–1948) visited LaGrange, he attracted the attention of local teenage girls who hoped they might be discovered as Hollywood's next movie star. His family roots run deep in Oldham County, from pioneer days, and he often came back throughout his life, even during the height of his career. He bought a house in LaGrange for his mother, Mary Oglesby Griffith, who died in 1915, but he kept the home for relatives and lived there briefly during the 1930s with his third wife, Evelyn Baldwin, while working on his autobiography. One of his distant cousins, Richard James Oglesby (1824–1899), was a three-term governor in Illinois with close ties to Abraham Lincoln.

When Griffith produced the epic film *The Birth of a Nation* (1915), it included massive battle scenes and large-scale sets that had never been seen before by film audiences, who, up until this time, were used to short films that lasted eight to ten minutes. *Birth of a Nation* was based on a novel, *The Clansman*, written by Tom Dixon Jr. It was set in the South during the Civil War and Reconstruction period, and it idolized the Ku Klux Klan as the home guard against the despised carpetbaggers and scallywags. This film is a classic study for those interested in American history, the civil rights movement and cinematography and the visual arts. In 1953, the Directors Guild of America established the D.W. Griffith Award, which was renamed in 1999 by the guild because of the "intolerable racial stereotypes" that appeared in *The Birth of a Nation*.

Griffith's grave is at the Mount Tabor Cemetery, not far from his family's farm. It is a marble slab that is surrounded by a small picket fence. About forty feet away from his monument is the grave site of his parents, Jacob and Mary Griffith. D.W. purchased a large monument on their site with an elaborate description of his father's military service.

This unusual epitaph gives insight to D.W. Griffith's passion and worldview that produced his epic film *The Birth of a Nation*. According to biographer Richard Scheckel in his book *D.W. Griffith: An American Life* (1984), Griffith idolized his father. In fact, D.W. Griffith stated that "the one person I really

Special Homes

Above: D.W. Griffith bought this home around 1915 for his mother, who died a few years later. He kept the house and lived there briefly during the 1930s when writing his autobiography. *Author's collection*.

Left: Richard Reynolds with his wife, Mary. Reynolds was a chauffeur for D.W. Griffith, and Mary was a teacher at the LaGrange Training School. *Oldham County Historical Society*.

loved most in all my life was my father." However, Jacob Griffith was not remembered as a nurturer or having a particularly good relationship with his children and wife. Instead, he was said to have had bursts of self-destruction, boozing and gambling away money, earning nicknames such as Thunder Jake and Roaring Jake. To Jacob's credit, he was also recognized as a gallant soldier, and he rose to the occasions of bravery when leading his troops. It seemed that he was at his best in situations that tested his courage. After the war, he would often recall his life as a soldier, reminiscing about the danger, hardships, camaraderie and gallantry of the Confederacy, romanticizing tales of battles in boozy settings with friends as D.W. sat close by. Jacob died when D.W. was ten years old.

D.W. Griffith took these tales from the father he idolized and saw the opportunity to spin them into the first epic film, *The Birth of a Nation*. When asked in later years, he admitted the film was a tribute to his father's life and the brave souls who lost their homeland to the carpetbaggers and scallywags that followed the Reconstruction period. The stereotypes of the Ku Klux Klan, African Americans and white Unionists that Griffith created in this film caused him to lose his place of recognition as America's father of the modern film industry. Although Griffith produced seminal film works, it was *The Birth of a Nation* that marked his career. Orson Welles said, "I have never really hated Hollywood except for its treatment of D.W. Griffith. No town, no industry, no profession, no art form owes so much to a single man."

On a local level, Griffith is remembered with some fondness and nostalgia. Ruby Duncan, who married D.W. Griffith's nephew, remembers seeing him in LaGrange when she was a little girl:

> Then came the most vivid memory of all. I lived at the corner of Washington and Cedar Streets. It was a chilly autumn evening. Just about twilight. Leaves were falling. There were several of us that decided we would roast potatoes in the culvert. We gathered some leaves and started a little fire in the culvert. Smoke was curling up, and we put the potatoes in the leaves to roast. Then we noticed two men coming down the street. One man was white, the other Black. The white man was dressed to perfection down to the spats over his shoes and a fancy cane in his hand. He had a notepad and pencil. They stopped to talk to us. He wanted to know what we were doing. He wrote it all down and laughed with us some. They then walked on down the sidewalk toward the cemetery. Mother came out to the front porch and called me in to supper. She said, "That was D.W. Griffith, the movie director, and Dick Reynolds, and you kids may be in the movies." I never

made a movie, but *I did marry D.W.'s great-nephew Tommy Duncan. The culvert and house are still there. Even now when I smell leaves burning, I think of that evening in autumn.*

Nancy Oglesby (1921–2018) met her cousin several times when she was a young girl at family get-togethers:

My dad and D.W. Griffith were double cousins. When I was in the seventh or eighth grade, he [D.W.] came to our house and brought his girlfriend and her mother with him, and everyone thought the mother was his girlfriend, but my mother said no, it is the daughter. Mother was right! She [D.W.'s girlfriend] was so pretty! I remember the first time I saw her, I couldn't take my eyes off her! She had on a blue dress and blue hat, and she was blonde. He gave me $5 and told me to go to the grocery to get some coffee—and he said to keep the change! That was the first time I ever had that much money. The coffee was twenty cents a pound, so I got quite a bit. He gave my dad $200 and my mother $100. It wasn't long after that they got married at the Brown Hotel. They moved back to the house I was born in. They had us for dinner for Thanksgiving, and they showed us movies. They were silent films. D.W. wanted to take my older sister to Hollywood and put her in the movies. But my mother let him know right away that wasn't going to happen.

D.W. and my dad teased each other all the time. I remember one time my dad told him, "I never did mind cutting your hair in the summertime because I could rest in the shade of your nose!"

Richard Reynolds's father, Richard S. Reynolds (1902–1973), was employed by D.W. Griffith. He lived briefly in Hollywood and took his wife, Mary, and his mother-in law with him. The younger Reynolds recalled:

My dad became D.W. Griffith's chauffeur, and then dad, mother and grandmother all moved to Los Angeles. My mother worked as a maid for Loretta Young. Daddy didn't talk much about Mr. Griffith, and growing up, I didn't know anything about Birth of a Nation. *Daddy said Griffith changed as he got older and wasn't as racist. Griffith didn't know how to drive a car, so he depended on Dad to drive. They toured the whole country. Daddy taught D.W. to drive when they returned to Kentucky. KET did a documentary on Griffith, and at the end of the film, they talked about Dad. Dad drove the hearse when they had Griffith's funeral in Oldham County.*

When Griffith died in 1948, his funeral was held at the Hollywood Masonic Temple, and then his body was flown back to lay in state at the Peak Funeral Home in LaGrange before his funeral at the Mount Tabor Cemetery. Over three hundred people attended the funeral in Hollywood, and many movie stars came to the graveside burial at Mount Tabor. Local native Georgia Hampton attended the funeral:

> *One of the biggest events I remember was the funeral of D.W. Griffith, the movie director. That was around 1949, and they brought him from Hollywood to be buried here in his native Oldham County. I went to the funeral (which was held at his family grave site in Centerfield at the Mount Tabor Methodist Church). I got to see movie actors Mary Pickford, Lillian Gish and Douglas Fairbanks Jr. There were movie cameras there.*

The Oldham County History Center at 106 North Second Street in LaGrange shows D.W. Griffith movies in the Peyton Samuel Head Theatre. There are personal items of Griffith's donated by family members, along with timelines and exhibits about his film. I often receive calls and we have visits at the history center from people who admire his work and are researching his life. Many people come just to view the select films of his we offer. Often, when giving tours of his grave, there will be Confederate flags among roses or poetry placed at his gravestone, which evokes the controversy of his life's accomplishments.

Risley-Head House: 108 North Second Street

This elaborate Victorian house started as a one-story home built by I.T Risley. Samuel Peyton Head purchased the home in the 1870s and added large two-story additions, Queen Anne detailing and the large wraparound porch. The original root cellar to the house in the back has been restored. The original carriage steps used to assist persons in boarding horse-drawn carriages are still in place on the Second Street side of the home.

Peyton Samuel Head (1849–1928) was born in Oldham County, the second son of James Madison Head (1812–1871) and Margaret McMakin (1827–1854). Peyton married Blanche Hitt Head (1867–1951), and they had three daughters: Louise Head Duncan (1891–1990), Frances Head Alley (1895–1981) and Margaret Head Gaines (1901–1982).

Special Homes

The Peyton Samuel Head house, 108 North Second Avenue, built in the 1840s with additions over the years. There is a root cellar structure in the backyard. *Oldham County Historical Society.*

Peyton Head was educated in LaGrange and at the Kentucky Masonic College. He began a career in real estate, which became his main course of work. He was appointed commissioner to settle estates and acted as arbitrator for failing businesses. He became a local business leader and helped establish Oldham Bank, which later became the Bank of Oldham County. He was the largest stockholder for the bank.

Peyton served at one time as deputy sheriff and shot and killed a man, in self-defense, when making an arrest. He also served as treasurer on the board of trustees for the City of LaGrange. He bought the house at 108 North Second as his "town" home, but he also owned a large farm near Ballardsville. One of his favorite pastimes was raising hound dogs for hunting.

Peyton's daughter Louise Head Duncan inherited the family home in LaGrange, where she spent most of her life. She was a very talented artist.

She attended Molly Mahan's private school in LaGrange at 116 East Main and the LaGrange Funk Seminary School through grade eight. She completed high school in Louisville and then went to Carmen Hagerman College in Lexington. She became the treasurer for Oldham County for ten years during the 1930s. She met her second husband, Curt Duncan, and they lived on their family farm during the summer in Ballardsville and wintered in the family home in LaGrange.

Louise Duncan was very charitable and supported many local organizations. She died in 1990 and left $5 million in a trust that became known as the Peyton Samuel Head Trust, which has distributed millions of dollars to Oldham County projects since her death. The distributions of the funds state, "The purposes for which these funds are used should in general add to the overall improvement of the quality of life of the people of Oldham County."

After Louise's death, she left her home at 108 North Second and a second house at 106 North Second to the Oldham County Historical Society. Her home is now the Peyton Samuel Head Family Museum, and the 106 North Second Street home is the J.C. Barnett Library and Archives on the Oldham County History Center campus.

James and Amanda Mount House: 106 North Second Avenue

When I started my job as the executive director at the Oldham County History Center 2004, we had just received a donation from Lucretia Davenport of a box of letters, receipts and family papers. Known as Grandma Railey's Box, this collection had been passed down through generations. Lucretia's husband, John Mount, had inherited the box, and after his death, Lucretia wanted to find an appropriate "home" for this rare collection. There was a set of thirty-two letters written by Amos Mount to his aunt Amanda in which he described his experiences during his journey as a Union soldier. Amos was seriously injured at Woodbury, near Murfreesboro, Tennessee, in 1863, but he survived, recovered and returned home to his beloved aunt Amanda. Later, he married and moved to Illinois.

When Lucretia came to donate Grandma Railey's Box to the Oldham County History Center, she did not know that our J.C. Barnett Library and Archives was once the home of James and Amanda Mount. As part of our collection today, these letters are important research materials to the life and culture of LaGrange during antebellum years.

The letters and documents of the Railey Box show the Mounts bought and sold slaves up to and through the Civil War. As early as 1843, there is a bill of sale that indicates James Mount purchased two enslaved people by the names of Jeremiah and Lucy Jane for $500. In April 1846, a receipt shows James Mount purchased a slave named William for $396 from William D. Mitchell, master in Chancery Court of Oldham County. A receipt dated April 12, 1848, from James Mount to J.J. Railey (brother of Amanda Railey Mount) details the payment for slaves who were part of Joseph Railey's (father of Amanda Railey Mount) estate in the amount of $465. Later, a receipt dated November 22, 1859, shows Amanda Railey Mount bought a slave named George for $1,250.

Not only do these documents indicate that the Mounts bought and owned slaves, but later receipts and letters also show that slaves ran away from the Mount home. When President Abraham Lincoln issued the Emancipation Proclamation in January 1863, all slaves in the Confederacy were legally free, but this did not apply to Kentucky because Kentucky had declared for the Union. In 1864, Lincoln declared that any slave who enlisted for the Union would be given freedom as well as freedom for his family. A flood of Kentucky slaves rushed to enlist at Camp Nelson outside Nicholasville in Jessamine County and Camp Taylor in Louisville. Two receipts in the James and Amanda Mount collection indicate a blatant disregard for the law, as Amanda Mount is documented to have paid slave catchers twice to retrieve slaves who had gone to Louisville. The first of these, Amanda Railey Mount paid William S. Bennett fifteen dollars "for trouble, expense, and taking runaway Negro soldier" to Louisville from LaGrange. Another receipt from Amanda Mount to J.W. Cardwell and Co. (a company that wrote out contracts to make claims on enlisted runaways) states Amanda's claim for two slaves.

In addition to being a slave owner, James Mount served on the LaGrange Board of Trustees for some time and worked on the Jail Oversight Commission. In ads placed in a September 1862 issue of the *Louisville Journal*, James Mount announced the capture of three runaways who were being held in the Oldham County jail. Bounty hunters from Harney, Hughes and Co. wrote to James Mount on August 9, 1862, requesting payment for capturing slaves in the advertisement.

In 2016, the J.C. Barnett Library and Archives at the Oldham County History Center was designated by the National Park Service as part of the National Underground Railroad Network. The National Park Service defines the Underground Railroad as the first step an enslaved person makes toward their escape, so the bounty hunter documents, signed by Amanda Mount, demonstrate that first step.

In 2021, the Oldham County History Center renovated one of the rooms of the archives, named the Mount Parlor, to reflect the life of the Mounts in the 1850s. The room has carefully selected period antiques and contains copies of the Mount slave papers. In 2022, an oil portrait of Kentucky statesman Henry Clay, painted by portrait artist Joseph Bush (1793–1865), was added to the parlor to tell the story of the Mount family. Clay was known to have been good friends with the Mounts and visited the home several times.

The legacy of the enslaved demonstrates how important democracy is—and how equal opportunity is a right of our nation. It is the same struggle that continues to repeat itself over time. Amanda Mount opened her family up for inspection, and it actually gives us a moment to witness a period that often denies the sacrifice of so many who we have not thanked for their labor and lives for a world that promises opportunity and equal rights for everyone.

Part VII
Churches

DeHaven Baptist Church

One of the most beautiful churches in Oldham County is the DeHaven Baptist Church, located on the corner of Main and Third Streets in LaGrange. The church was named for its benefactor, Judge Samuel E. DeHaven (1826–1893). DeHaven was born in Jefferson County and attended the common schools in his neighborhood. At the age of fourteen, he went to Illinois for two years to work on a farm and then returned to Jefferson County, where he taught school for a couple of years. He enrolled in St. Joseph's College in Bardstown and graduated with a BA in 1848. DeHaven moved to Westport, in Oldham County, to teach school and studied law under a local barrister, George Armstrong. DeHaven was admitted to the Oldham County bar in 1850.

He was an ardent member of the Democratic Party and was in favor of the Union during the Civil War. He served in the Kentucky legislature in 1857–58 and was elected to the state senate to represent the counties of Henry, Oldham and Trimble, serving four years. He served as chairman of the finance committee while in the Senate and as chairman of the ways and means committee in the House. The period of his services in both branches of the legislature embraced the time in which stormy discussions occurred preceding the Civil War and during which all the war measures adopted by the state were inaugurated.

This LaGrange United Pentecostal Church at 206 East Washington Street was originally built for the Baptist congregation in 1870 before their move to the DeHaven Baptist Church on Third Street. *Author's collection.*

DeHaven practiced law in Oldham, Trimble, Henry, Shelby, Anderson, Spencer and Bullitt Counties. He ran for and was elected circuit judge in 1876 and continued his term as judge until his death in 1893. DeHaven helped to organize the Oldham Bank at LaGrange in May 1885 and became president of the board of directors. He had large landed interests in Oldham, Henry and Jefferson Counties and was actively engaged in farming operations in those counties, not hesitating to go into the field and labor himself when the occasion required.

Judge DeHaven didn't marry until he was fifty-seven years old. He married Betty Russell, from Oldham County, in 1883, and it was reported that he said, "Finally now I have time, so let's get married." When he died on November 28, 1893, at his residence in LaGrange, his body was transported to Cave Hill Cemetery in Louisville by a special train. Area judges were pallbearers at his funeral, and there is a very large life-size statue of him at the grave site.

A copy of DeHaven's will indicates his estate was worth $600,000, which was divided among his nieces and nephews. One of his faithful hired hands was allowed to choose a tract of land and a horse. Some funds were given to

Cave Hill Cemetery for the upkeep of the grave and statue. Nancy Oglesby (1921–1918) remembered her young years attending DeHaven:

> *I mainly remember going to church when I was a kid, DeHaven Memorial Baptist Church. I was practically born there and went to every mission there was—Sunday school, I even have a diploma from the Cradle Row Department. Mother's friends Helen Bowman and Harold Snook and his mother lived up past us and would meet us at the corner (at the Courts), and we all walked to church. On New Year's Eve, we would go to church about nine at night and play games and they had refreshments. At midnight, we would go in the sanctuary and hold hands and sing songs. There were also hymn sings, and we would go visit different churches.*

First Baptist Church of LaGrange

In 1867, Black members of the LaGrange Baptist Church desired to organize a church of their own, whereupon letters of dismissal were granted them and a substation start in moneys was given them with which to erect a building. The church was organized and located on Cedar Street. Reverends Warren Lewis, Braxton and Thomas of Lexington; Reverend Elijah P. Marrs of Shelbyville; and Brother Joe Davis, Ben Coomes, Pete Parker and Lee Woodfork served as the church organizers. The trustees listed on the lien for the property were Palmer Berry, Abram Riley and Dennis Roberts.

Elijah Marrs was a member of the association of the State Convention of Colored Baptist Churches, which was organized in 1865. This association, initially composed of twelve Black Baptist churches from across Kentucky, came together to support public and religious education initiatives, and by 1869, there were over 12,260 members representing over twenty-seven churches. Through Elijah Marrs and his brother H.C. Marrs, the First Baptist Church received funds from the Freedmen's Bureau to help with the education of the children in the community.

Richard Reynolds (1857–1933) was another important minister at this church who helped construct a new building at Sauer and First Streets and grow the church to two hundred members during his sixteen years as pastor. Reynolds was a good friend of the Reverend W.H. Craighead (1861–1940), an Oldham County native, whose parents were enslaved by John Martin Taylor at Westport.

The First Baptist Church, on the corner of Saurer and Highway 53 North, circa 1870s, where Elijah Marrs taught Black children after the Civil War. It is no longer extant. *Oldham County Historical Society*.

Craighead's education began from the efforts of Elijah and H.C. Marrs at the First Baptist Church in LaGrange. Craighead moved to Louisville at the age of twenty-five and became one of the first four Black men to graduate from the State University College Department (again, a college that was established through the efforts of Elijah Marrs and later became Simmons University).

Craighead became minister of the Zion Baptist Church in Louisville. This was a prestigious church whose ministers in the future included A.D. Williams King, Martin Luther King's brother. Craighead was minister at Zion for forty-five years and grew the membership to 1,200. He served on national boards for the Baptist Conventions, started the first Negro Boy Scout troop in Louisville and secured homes for orphaned children.

In May 1971, the congregation moved to a building of the former LaGrange Training School, and the original church was torn down. Reverend Tunstill came to the church in 1974 and has remained since, leading the church through various stages of development. The old school building burned in 1990, and the church rebuilt a new building on the same site where the congregation remains today. In 2014, the Oldham County Historical Society placed a Kentucky Historical Marker on the property to mark the site's history as one of the original Rosenwald Schools in Kentucky.

Harry Booker grew up during the 1950s, and his grandmother Hattie Booker took him to the First Baptist Church every Sunday, as Harry recalled:

> *She* [Hattie Booker] *was strict, strict, strict, church, church, church. All day Sunday we went to church, at the First Baptist Church, on the corner of Sauer and First, across from Herb Hendron's store. We used to have basket days back in those days or homecoming. We had dinners, tables and stuff outside, fried chicken, lot of singing, lot of preaching all afternoon. Some inside, some outside, world of stuff going on. Ice cream, anything you'd want to eat.*
>
> *We had BTU training on Sunday night. That was Bible class. They had night service too. We were at church all the time on Sunday. Never went home. After Hattie died, I still went to church. I'm not a Saint now, but church means a whole lot to me. I just have a desire to go because I am hungry to go for the word of God; it means a whole lot to you. You will be a better person, better character. I feel bad a lot of times and think I'm not going to church, but when I go, I get to feeling better. People look up to you more, and I wouldn't ever get nowhere today if it hadn't been for the love of Hattie and her keeping the tight reins on me. It* [church] *soothes my appetite and suited taste better and believe the Lord blesses me more, it means a lot for me to do the right direction, everybody respects you, cares for you, do for you. I wouldn't have a thing in the world if it weren't for church and those who care.*

LaGrange Presbyterian Church

The LaGrange Presbyterian Church at 207 West Jefferson was built in 1880 on a lot given by Amanda Mount (1810–1888). Amanda and her husband, James, lived around the block from the church at 106 North Second Street, which is now the J.C. Barnett Library and Archives of the Oldham County History Center, designated by the National Park Service as part of the National Underground Railroad Network. It was also Masonic poet and scholar Dr. Rob Morris's (1818–1888) church, of which he declared, "There are two things dear to my heart, my Presbyterian Church and Freemasonry."

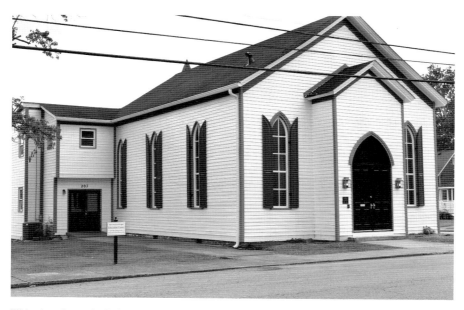

This church was built in 1880 as a Presbyterian church where Dr. Rob Morris composed hymns and recited poetry. *Author's collection.*

When Amanda deeded the lot to the Presbytery, Rob Morris was listed on the deed along with the Louisville Presbytery, John Swain, Richard T. Jacob, David Johnson and Elders.

Today, the church serves as the Rob Morris Chapel Education Building for the Oldham County History Center. It was renovated by the history center in 2006 with funds from the Kentucky Department of Transportation and Samuel Peyton Head Trust. The renovation included returning the structure back to its high arched mahogany windows and returning the indoor ceiling of the chapel to its original height, creating a nice effect for music and presentations. The original building in 1880 was erected by a Louisville contractor with the principal work done by local townsman Frank Carter.

In 1949, the Presbyterian church closed its doors due to few members. The following years, it served as rental space, and then the Church of Christ occupied the building until the late 1990s. The Oldham County History Center bought the building in 2000 and added it as part of its campus, and today, it serves as an event and activity center.

LaGrange Methodist Church

A large mural graced the altar of the LaGrange Methodist Church, where I was baptized and a member during my childhood and early adult years. The thirty-foot-high mural depicted Christ holding a lamb surrounded by a flock of sheep amid a pastoral scene like the landscape of rural Oldham County. When I was a child, the mural gave me a place to digress as the sermons tended to linger.

To add interest to the mural, a story was passed down through the decades about its origin. Mary Virginia Manby (1906–1992) wrote a history on the Methodist church that included a story about the mysterious artist:

> When the Sanctuary was being redecorated a stranger came by, stopped and asked for work. The contractor being in need of a painter hired him. After viewing the Sanctuary, the stranger asked permission to paint a picture on the blank wall behind the pulpit. After conferring with the pastor and the board he was given permission to paint, The Good Shepherd. From a small Sunday School picture card, he produced a work of art that bespoke the fact that this man, a wanderer, possessed ability and skill that could have rated him among the artists of the day. In appreciation of his ability two ladies

AME LaGrange Methodist Church beside the Kentucky Masonic College, circa 1890, at the intersection of First Street and Jefferson. *Oldham County Historical Society.*

of the church gave him $35 in addition to his wages. It was said that shortly after finishing the painting, officers came and took him to California where he was charged with a crime. At the LaGrange Methodist Church he will always remain "The Stranger." We never knew his name.

We now know that *The Good Shepherd* is the piece the stranger reproduced, originally created by Bernard Plockhurst (1825–1907), a German artist who became noted for his large paintings of religious themed subjects. Plockhurst's piece *The Good Shepherd* has been popular with American Christian groups and repeatedly used in numerous formats.

When the church was sold, the mural could not be removed since it is painted on plaster. It now stands behind a walled storage closet. When I went to inspect the mural, I found it still in good shape, and it brought back a flood of memorable events that took place when I was a member there. Inspection of the mural revealed that it was signed and dated, contrary to Mrs. Manby's statement. The artist was D.H. Woolridge, 1905. I investigated the name but could not find any further clues to the artist and what became of him.

The church history begins in 1842. It was initially a framed traditional-style, one-room frame building with a double door on each side of the front of the building. Men entered on the right side, women on the left. To the right of the pulpit was an "amen" corner.

On November 10, 1889, a new brick sanctuary was built. It was heated with a coal furnace and had new light fixtures and contemporary oil chandeliers. The elaborate stained-glass arch windows were installed on three sides of the brick church. There was an indebtedness of $1,300 on the new building. To help liquidate the debt, the youth of the church sold bricks throughout the community.

One of the more famous pastors was the Reverend George Froh, who was pastor from 1895 to 1899. Froh was a captain in the Union army and a native of Germany. He commanded a unit of German-speaking troops during the Civil War.

During the 1950s and '60s, Brad Clifford attended the Methodist church. His mother was the church secretary, and he has fond recollections of his experiences going to church:

We were real involved with the LaGrange Methodist Church. I was an acolyte. You meet, get a good foundation for how to live your life. I went to church until I graduated from high school. I wouldn't change it for anything in the world. We had youth groups; we would rake leaves to make money for our youth group, deliver food baskets around the holiday season. We went to church every Sunday. Dad was responsible for making coffee at the church, so we would get there early. Toughest thing about going to church was Mom made us wear a tie! We would play ping pong while Dad made coffee. There were great men in the church. Brother Kerce, our preacher, was the minister then. He was a storyteller. Charlie Robinson was my Sunday school teacher; he had me for three or four years. Elsie Smith was also a Sunday school teacher, and Mr. Kincaid was one of the nicest guys I have ever known. Raymond Wilborn—he always had a joke for us.

The men would have a pancake prayer breakfast every Saturday, and all the men could cook. Dad would get us up early Saturday—he helped with breakfast—we got eggs, sausage, biscuits, gravy. Food was excellent; all those men could cook. There was potluck on Sunday nights.

The church was sold and bought by Fiscal Court in the 1980s. Today, it serves as an office building for several county government agencies.

LaGrange Kynett Methodist Episcopal Church

The LaGrange Kynett Methodist Episcopal Church's charter was created shortly after the Civil War. The church building still stands and has functioned as various businesses over the years. Many local African American leaders—such as Washington Bullitt, Henry Vance, Benjamin Thomas, Jonas Smith, Willis Jordan, Henry Terrell, James Coons and James Ford—served as trustees for the Methodist church to establish its place in the LaGrange community. The first transaction for establishing the church site comes from the following:

This indenture made and enclosed unto this 7th day of April 1868 by and between Susan Bennett of the town of LaGrange County of Oldham and State of Kentucky on the first part and Henry Vance, Benjamin Thomas and Jonas Smith (men of color) sole Trustees of the Methodist Colored Church of LaGrange of the second part. Witnesseth that the said party of the first part for and in consideration of the sum of Fifty Dollars cash in hand paid the receipts which is hereby acknowledged.

Have granted, bargained and sold and by these presents does grant bargain convey unto the said party of the second part as Trustees of the

The Kynett Methodist Church (circa 1868) was established by local civil rights advocates shortly after the Civil War. *Oldham County Historical Society.*

The Kynett Methodist Church congregation, circa 1950s. *Harris Collection, Oldham County Historical Society.*

> *said Methodist Colored Church and to their successors in office as Trustees for said church part of the South East corner of Lot No. 5 lying and being in the town of LaGrange fronting on Monroe and South Streets said lots of ground fronts forty feet on Monroe Street and Sixty feet on South Street. To have and to hold the aforesaid lot of ground unto the party of the second part as trustees for the said church and to their successors in office for the sole use benefit and behalf of the said church and the title to the said lot with all the opportunities as thereunto belonging the party of the first part will warrant and defined free from the claims of all persons whomsoever.*
>
> *In testimony where of the said Susan Bennett party of the first part has hereunto set her hand this day and herein written.*
>
> William Taylor   Susan Bennett

Later, in 1894, the trustees of the church paid off a loan of $130 to Peyton Samuel Head to secure "the church building or meeting house, pulpit or desk, pews, benches and all other church furniture."

Frances Walters's husband was a preacher at Kynett. She recalls their experiences at the church:

> *My husband, Walter Walters, was a minister at the Kynett Methodist Church. We got married in Clarksville. My parents didn't know about it! I met Rev on the corner up by Cassady's when I got off work. I think it was love at first sight; I sat on the front pews so he would see me. People that went to that church were Mattie Pearl Browning, Ida Mae Beaumont, Lucille Beaumont, Cora Bullitt Harris, Nathan Posey, Benjamin Browning, George Browning, Robert Elzy and so many I can't think of them all.*
>
> *We were always inviting people to church. We had basket dinners where everyone fixed a basket and you would give a donation to the church to get a basket. A good basket would have fried chicken, mashed potatoes, corn pudding, green beans and a cake or pie and maybe homemade dinner rolls or cornbread. The church supplied the drinks. We would eat out on the grounds behind the church. There was the parsonage there.*

Diane Booker went to Kynett with her mother when she was a little girl:

> *Dad went to the Baptist church in Shelby County, where I go now. Mother went to Kynett Methodist in LaGrange. On prayer night, I went with my dad because Mom worked at night. We always had to go to Sunday school; it was fun. Cousin Lizzie made it fun. We had these little cards*

with verses to memorize, and she had Christmas and Easter plays. We would dye eggs for Easter and fill bags of candy for Santa Claus during Christmas. In the summer, we had a basket meeting. They would have food, and a preacher would come from somewhere else and preach. It was all day. Everyone would cook and bring dishes. And everyone you ever knew would come; a lot of people lived out on farms, so you may not see them but at the basket meeting. Mr. Posey, he would have ice cream, the bar ice cream—Neapolitan: strawberry, vanilla and chocolate. And he would treat the children to those at the basket meeting.

Church took all day every Sunday. You went to Sunday school, church, go home and eat and come back in the evening. Usually, church service would last an hour or hour and a half. My great-grandmother's brother Henry would ring the bell every Sunday to let people know it was time to go to church.

I started singing in the Kynett Methodist Church choir in the '70s. And our choir began to travel a lot around the state: Horse Cave, Cynthiana, the Methodist Convention in East Kentucky, the courthouse yard, a lot of different places. Some of the people in the choir were Ida Beaumont, Millie Arnold, Carolyn Browning, Shirley Browning, Lettie Goldsmith, Ann Goldsmith, Della Murphy, Nadine Elzy, Frances Walters and Barbara Browning, and Wayne Green was our pianist. My favorite gospel music is "Walk Around Heaven All Day." Shirley would sing "I Don't Know Who Holds Tomorrow." "Joy," "Yes Lord, Yes Lord, My Soul Says Yes, Yes" and "A Closer Walk with Me" are some other songs that we sung a lot.

The Kynett Methodist Church continued its tenure serving the African American population until it merged with the LaGrange United Methodist Church in 1995. The new congregation abandoned both the LaGrange United Methodist Church building on Jefferson Street (circa 1888) and the Kynett Methodist Church building (circa 1868) on Second Street and constructed a church on Highway 146 on the west side of LaGrange.

LaGrange Christian Church

The LaGrange Christian Church was organized in 1845. It originally met twice a month in a small building owned by the Masonic Lodge. In 1866, a new church was built on Jefferson Street between Walnut and First Streets. The congregation built the church on its current site and opened in

Left: World War II soldier Paul Snyder, Battery C, First Platoon, gun squad, died in a ground assault in a small French-occupied village, driving back German troops. *Oldham County Historical Society*.

Right: World War II soldier gunner Earl Bennett died retrieving food for fellow soldiers after their B-47 was shot down in occupied France. *Oldham County Historical Society*.

1936 with its front door facing First Street. In 1954, the church remodeled and enlarged, moving the entrance to the side of the church, where it remains today.

The stories of Paul Snyder and Earl Bennett are intricately linked to the LaGrange Christian Church and seem to be another serendipitous incident for me from my work at the Oldham County History Center. Their connections were discovered through the donation of Paul Snyder's World War II artifacts by his niece Peggy Burge and from the donation of a scrapbook on Earl Bennett by history center member Gene Crady.

Paul Snyder and Earl Bennett attended the LaGrange Christian Church throughout their young lives. Paul was born in 1919, and Earl was born in 1923. Though four years apart, they had a lot of similarities. They were friends at their church, attending the same Sunday school classes. They were handsome young men, both described as tall and lanky. Both had a good sense of humor. They also lost their lives, killed in action, on the same day, June 14, 1944, eight days after the D-day invasion in German-occupied France, within one hundred miles of each other.

Paul's family lived in LaGrange: his parents, Mr. and Mrs. R.H. Snyder; sister, Margaret; half sister, Gladys; and brother, Robert. Paul attended LaGrange High School, where there were thirty-six students in his senior class. The 1937 LaGrange High School yearbook provides this tribute to Paul:

There is a Snyder boy; they call him Paul.
On account of his ambition, he'll soar above all.
When asked what he intends to be, Paul did say,
I'm going to be President of the USA

Paul always moves with a lagging step;
He doesn't have a lot of pep,
And yet he's always ready to go
When anyone can a good time show.

A bright red curly head he possesses;
That he has a temper he confesses.
But his anger one cannot easily provoke
He can even take Mr. Trapp's mean joke.

His class will stated:

Name: Paul Button Snyder
Pastime: Eating
Favorite Expression: Ain't
Ambition: Marry Rich

Earl Bennett grew up on his family farm and attended Liberty High School, where he graduated in 1941. Liberty was a rural school with fifteen students in Earl's class. Like Paul, Earl was a popular student; he was in Future Farmers of America, the Science Club, the Dramatic Club and Booster Club and was manager of the Basketball Club. In the class will, Earl's "dramatic ability" is compared to Clark Gable, and his class prophecy suggests that the future Earl Bennett will be a Baptist minister. Earl's parents were Helen and Earl Bennett. He had a sister, Mary Elizabeth; brother, Clarence; and half brother, Lindsey.

Paul enlisted in the U.S. Army on February 16, 1942. He was part of Battery C, First Platoon, First Gun Squad. His crew entered a small French village to drive back the Germans. The gun crew was knocked out by a German tank and mortar shelling. The crew was fired on before their 57mm gun was set up. Four men were killed, four wounded. The four killed that day were Corporal Snyder, Corporal Apicella, Private Husk and Sergeant Wilson. A photo of the aftermath was taken by Robert Capa and appeared in *Life* magazine on July 3, 1944. Paul was buried with fellow soldiers at the St. Laurent Cemetery at Omaha Beach in France.

Earl's military history was captured by his mother, who created a scrapbook on him. It contained a series of letters and v-mail written by Earl, along with newspaper articles and military information regarding Earl's life and death on the battlefield.

Earl Bennett enlisted the same year as Paul, in 1942. Earl joined the U.S. Army Air Corps and began his life as a soldier. Over the next two years, Earl honed his skills as an engineer gunner and was assigned to the 640th Bomb Squad, 409th Bomb Group. His pilot was Leon Cohen, Staff Sergeant Logan Young was the turret gunner and Earl was the tail gunner on a B-47.

A year after Earl's death, Mrs. Bennett received the following letter from Elsie Young that describes the last few days of Bennett's life and what happened with his crew members. Elsie was the mother of Staff Sergeant Logan Young, who was the front runner.

> *August 22, 1945*
> *Dear Mrs. Bennett:*
> *The night Logan arrived home, we sat up until after 3:30 a.m. for he wanted to tell me everything about the experience a year ago last June and I will try to tell you as much as I can remember about it, for do not like to ask Logan any details for awhile, for he is gradually trying to forget it as he settles into civilian life again.*
>
> *You probably know already that the tail was shot off of the plane and the men crash landed in a swamp behind the lines in No Man's Land after dropping their bombs on the target. They went down in a little valley that was surrounded with farms all over the hillsides, except for one level place that the Germans had covered with tall poles strung with high tension wires to catch the men parachuting down....*
>
> [After being shot down in the plane] *they escaped to the tall grass in the fields that first night. (There was also a large German gun in the field.)*
>
> *The next morning, they buried the parachute they had taken for cover, they hid emergency rations alongside of a hedge row, for they figured they could go back to them later....* [Eventually] *they were able to solicit an*

old French couple who tried to help them, but who had to be so very careful of being discovered for the Germans were everywhere. The old lady helped them to an old bread kiln just large enough to have one man lying on his back and one on his side at a time and the third on a little shelf at one end. The main problem was in trying to carry a small pan of milk to the men, for any food that went out that way would attract attention, but she did manage to carry a little milk and a small bottle of cider to the boys.

Toward the end of the third day, the men were nearly starved from the shock of the landing, being soaked to the skin all that time and no sleep. Logan and Earl were side by side near the door and Lee was on the shelf and all but Earl dozed off for a minute. Logan said that suddenly he was wide awake and realized that one of them was not there and he put his hand over to feel for Earl whose turn was near the door. Earl was gone and Logan thought perhaps he had crawled around the corner of the kiln where the men went to the toilet. Finally, he whispered to Lee to see if he had heard Earl crawl out. They waited a little while and suddenly the big gun opened, then a rifle report, another big gun, and another rifle report. Lee and Logan knew then what had happened. Earl had gone back to try to get the rations they had hid and as near as they could figure out when they went to him after they were finally rescued; poor Earl never knew what hit him.

The French all left the place after Earl was killed and that left the boys without any help whatever. They left the kiln a few minutes before twenty Germans with big anti-aircraft guns moved in and set the guns up in the back yard where the men had been. The next heartbreaking day was the eighth day when they knew they were done for, for the Americans were too far back to reach them.... They tried to dig their own grave close to a road so that when the Americans did reach the point, they could notify their families. It took them all day to dig the grave just deep enough for one man to lie flat and the other on his side and deep enough to be level with the ground around. They crawled in waiting for unconsciousness to relieve them of the hunger, pain in their feet and the terrible chill.... During the ninth night there was a lot of activity in the air.... [They were befriended again] by another man and his wife who took them into their home and told them that paratroopers had landed but that Germans were still everywhere.... [Americans landed, and they were finally rescued the next day.] Leon and Logan led the American soldiers back to where Earl was. Then the officers had to hold them back, for they started to go to him and the officers felt that the Germans had planted a mine under where he was laying.... But they promised to take proper care of him.

Earl's remains were sent back to LaGrange, and he was buried at the Valley of Rest Cemetery. He was the first of Oldham County's sons who died in World War II and returned for interment.

The Immaculate Conception Church

The first Catholic church in LaGrange was built in 1875 in response to the influx of Irish Catholics who worked for the L&N Railroad. The original church site is a vacant lot on the north side between First and Second Streets on Madison. It seated three hundred people. In 1899, when the railroad moved its main operations from LaGrange to Louisville, many of the church members moved back to Louisville. The first church was torn down, and a much smaller church was constructed on the same site in 1900. As membership began to grow, the Immaculate Conception Church was built on Fifth Street in 1950. This site was once used as a football field for Funk Seminary High School after the Civil War. In 1927, the site was used for the Centennial Celebration of LaGrange.

Immaculate Conception included a small private school. Paulette Gibson Carey recalled her years there as a student:

> *I started first grade at Immaculate Conception School in LaGrange. We only had two classrooms, four grades in each room. Sister Mary Coletta taught first through fourth; Sister Mary Victoria was principal and taught grades five through eight. The nuns traveled by city bus from St. Aloysius in Pewee Valley.*
>
> *Other families at Immaculate Conception were the Kinsers, Kamers, Greenwells, Dietrichs, Drurys, Allgeiers, Vittitows, Coopers, Kings, Walshes and Osborns and more that I can't remember.*
>
> *Father Albert Schmidt and Father William Dierson were the earliest priests, and Mrs. Mottman of Anita Springs was our guardian angel. She gave us kids parties and gifts on every holiday and special occasion. She also played the organ for our school and church.*

The Immaculate Conception school closed in 2006. A new school, St. Mary's Academy, opened in Jefferson County in 2007 as its replacement. The Immaculate Conception Church has built a new sanctuary and enlarged its building on the original site as the congregation has continued to grow.

Part VIII

Main Street LaGrange

Main Street in LaGrange is well known for the railroad tracks that were laid down in 1851. This remains an active railroad line, running mainly freight through town. Although LaGrange is not the only town in the world today with an active rail line through its center, it is one of the few remaining in the United States. As one can only imagine, the people, businesses and train have been intricately connected through stories and experiences since the mid-1800s. In the following sections, I have included some reminiscences by people and their experiences on Main Street, followed by short histories and stories of some of the businesses over the years.

Main Street Recollections

J.W. Hall

There were four grocery stores in LaGrange. I would sit on the porch swing and talk to Mr. and Mrs. Peak at Peak's Funeral Home on Main Street. Mrs. Peak knew a lot of history. She would sit on the swing, and I would join her (as a little boy), and she would tell me about the history. We would watch people come in town, and there were about three or four people that would come in town still using horse and buggy. I would go to the picture show across the street. We would go to the show and watch the show when

Main Street LaGrange

Jones Downey Parade on Main Street in LaGrange held in honor of Korean War veterans. *Oldham County Historical Society*.

An inside image of Mary Dee's Sweet Shop at 115 East Main, which was a popular hangout for teens in the 1930s and '40s. *Oldham County Historical Society*.

my parents went shopping in LaGrange. We always went to the candy store in MacKenzie's. We could buy a lot of candy for a nickel. I would buy coconut bonbons. Sometimes they would have apples dipped in caramel; that was quite a treat.

There was a horse stable on Washington Street. The Burgins had a stable down there, east of First Street. There was a creamery there too, Ardmore Creamery. Burgins had a dairy operation and [would] bring it there, and they would sell butter and cream and milk there. Mary Dee had a shop, and the drugstore sold sandwiches and Cokes, and Gatewoods, that was a drugstore down there by Karen's book barn today. The biggest department store was Rosenburg's department store. They always rode the streetcar from Louisville to LaGrange. They lived in Louisville. I remember that Mrs. Rosenburg walked about fifty feet in front of Mr. Rosenburg, and she would yell, "Al, you coming?"

Ida Mae Beaumont

[During segregation years,] we could go to the movies but had to sit up in the balcony. We couldn't drink out of the water fountain or sit on the courthouse lawn. You couldn't sit at the drugstore for a drink, but you could go in and get it. A lot of times you had to go through the back door.

Marjorie Morgan

My first job was in Glauber's Five and Dime Store, on Saturdays, when I was still in school. After I graduated, I was a telephone operator for LaGrange before I went to U of L in the fall. It [the telephone system] was called back then a drop system. There were little windows; if you rang your phone at home, this little latch let loose and a window dropped down and said what that number was that was calling from, and then you plugged into that and asked them what number they wanted, and they would tell you. And then you had to know where all these numbers were, and you took the other cord and plugged it in there and you rang it. And if it was a party line, there were so many longs and so many shorts. And then they talked. There were two of us up there all the time. Mrs. Jesse Lindsey was the chief operator. Elizabeth Roberts was one of the operators, and Amy Alice George Rogers was another one. It was upstairs, over the back part of Dizzy Dave's, I guess. Southern Bell I guess operated it.

Party lines meant there was more than one person on that number. If it was A, there was maybe one long ring, and if it was B, maybe two shorts.

Some of them had just one line, if it was a business. If you were on a party line and someone was talking on it, you could hear them talking. Say, 5180A was talking and you are 5180B, and you picked up your phone to make a phone call, you would hear these voices talking back and forth. And sometimes they would get irate if they thought someone was listening. And I think you could tell by the sound if someone picked up and was listening. And they would say, "We will be off in just a minute."

And when there was a fire, the fire alarm was a big tower that sat over in front of the old fire department, right out of the window from where we were working. If you had a fire, you called the exchange, and we went to a switch on the wall to set off the alarm. Of course, there were curious people then, like there is now, and they wanted to know where the fire was, if it was some of their friends or something. So, by the time you went over to that switch and turned that switch so the volunteers would come to get the fire engine, every drop on that board would be down where everybody had called in to see where that fire was! And you would just start down and punch down each one. So it was, I can still see that happening, I really can! But every drop would be down, and I thought, "Good grief!"

Barbara Hoffman

I remember where most the stores were when I was growing up. [Starting at the end of First Street and Main, going east,] *there was Jerry's Corner Store, Rosenburg's Department Store, then MacKenzie's, the Hat Shop, Barr's Grocery, Glauber's Ten Cent Store, Mary Dee's Sweet Shop, the next building I can't remember, then Griffith Theatre, Gatewood's Drugstore and the Masonic Building. Across the street there was Ballard's Department Store, Lucy's Beauty Shop, Peak's Funeral Home, there was a dime store where the Tattoo Shop is and there was a Kroger's next to drugstore. And there were some others I can't recollect. The Robertsons had a creamery behind Jerry's Corner Store, there on the corner of Washington and First.*

Martha Manby

They had dances above the hardware store, Kincaids; it was the T.W. Duncan store then. There were dances upstairs over that; there was live music.

When we came in LaGrange, we played cards. We went to the Mary Dee's Shop. It had booths down the walls and a big round table in back where we would gather and sit and gab. It was a sweet shop. You bought Cokes and sandwiches.

Mr. Tom Fils, who was a friend of Rush Gatewood's, was determined he was going to take me to Hollywood and D.W. Griffith was going to do things for me.

I met D.W. Griffith and one of his wives, later on in my life. He was a celebrity of course, and it was a treat to see someone like that. They used to come in Mary Dee's Shop, and that is probably where I first met him.

Harry Booker
The best dressed men in LaGrange were Milburn Wilson, Shirley McKenzie and Dick Ireland. I looked up to those men. Wilson was a surveyor, worked for the state. In LaGrange, down in the corner, [first floor of the Masonic Lodge], *that is where the pool hall was. Blacks couldn't go in there, but I could because Mr. Ireland knew me. Dick Ireland was the best pool player around. He never wore an old coat; he wore a stiff collared shirt, had a diamond ring. He worked for Rush Gatewood and played pool all his life. In them days, people didn't have much, so when people had things, you noticed. I would go up there and deliver ice, clean the place up, go up to Mary Dee's Thompson and bought cake and pies back.*

Everybody played horseshoes back in them days. The Beaumont boys were good at horseshoes. We played in people's backyard, Beaumont's backyard.... That was a game and a half back in them days; you played good horseshoes, you were a bad boy! You played good horseshoes, you could get a girlfriend!

Billie Clark
On Saturdays, we would bring our car up and park it around Head's Drug Store and then come back later and walk around and visit with everyone. LaGrange was packed. We used to go to Mundlochs and get an ice cream cone, and Daddy would never let us walk on the side of the street where Thompson's was because Daddy said that was a "beer joint." [This Thompson's Restaurant & Bar was a different restaurant than Mary Dee Thompson's Sweet Shop.] *At Halloween, we would always come up to the LaGrange gym. All the parents would furnish stuff for the kids. I remember one time I had long, black pigtails and I was Pocahontas.*

Mabel Tingle
I started working at the Townsend's Restaurant to work. Gracee was Mrs. Townsend's first name. They had plate lunches with hamburgers, things

like that. LaGrange was a busy place then [1944], specially on Saturday night. Theater was going, pool halls were going. People could go to Mrs. Thompson's saloon.

Barney Barnett
I could mow a couple of yards for two or three bucks, then go to the movies for fifty cents, get Milk Duds and a Coke. When it was over, you went to Sadies for an ice cream cone. Sadies was a restaurant on Main Street; there were pinball machines, Cokes were a nickel, ice cream was a nickel, and she had cheeseburgers and hamburgers, but we couldn't afford those very often. I didn't have that much money! Saturday nights were big in LaGrange. There was no place to park; it was full. Everyone came to town on Saturday night to do their grocery shopping.

I used to go to the pool hall. I went to Pete's Pool Hall. It was the best hamburger you could eat! My parents didn't really like it when I went to the pool hall, but they didn't know it. I remember the old interurban station on Main Street. I used to pick up the newspapers there for my paper route. I also got paid to read the water meters at people's houses. There was eight hundred water meters in town; I would do it in a day and a half, and I got ten cents a meter. Water came from Mac's Lake for LaGrange. Norman Allgeier worked there, and if you went out there on Sundays, you could clean your car because the water pressure was so much better.

Everybody in town knew your parents, and you could get in trouble for everything! By the time you got home, your parents knew if you did something you weren't supposed to. Throw a rock that you shouldn't have thrown, stuff like that.

Hugh Martin sits on a bar stool at Pete's Pool Hall in LaGrange at 119 West Main, circa 1960. *Oldham County Historical Society.*

115

Georgia Hampton

In 1955, if you bought so many groceries at the Kroger Store (by Inkwell Tattoos today), you could pay ninety-nine cents and get a cookbook that would tell you how to cook anything you wanted to cook. I still have that cookbook. Pete Leezer's garage was nearby Krogers, as was Doug Wise's barbershop, and then there was the Ballard Brothers Store. Back then, you knew everybody in LaGrange. I still have my hair fixed at Weible's Beauty Shop on Third Street. Barbara's place has been in operation fifty years; now it is only open on Thursday and Fridays.

Louise Morris

The Teen Club was a popular place to go. Trigg Black started the Teen Club back where Karen's Book Barn is today [the Masonic Lodge building]. *It was on Friday and Saturday nights from seven until ten. You went home early because you went to church the next day; all the kids went to church. Sometimes Friday it was movie night, and I saw my first,* Psycho, *and had nightmares for weeks. He had bands come from all over, and it was very well chaperoned. We danced our feet off. It was lined with chairs, but we never sat down much, and if there was any dirty dancing going on, they got thrown out of the Teen Club. Trigg was in my class and the son of Harold and Ruth Black. The bands were local. John Paul Staten played the drums, Jimmy Truman played, Steve Lindell. Seemed liked the Esquires played and maybe the Monarchs, when they first started. There wasn't any food. When John Paul played "Wipe-Out," everyone went nuts!*

Jimmy Oldson's Barber Shop

The barber pole sign hung outside this iconic barbershop at 204 East Main Street, which served customers for almost fifty years. Mr. Willard had the first barbershop (which was Owen Oglesby's butcher shop), and then Frank Wise bought out Willard, and the last barber was Jimmy Oldson. Jimmy reminisced about his business in the following from his Living Treasures Oral History at the Oldham County History Center.

The barbershop was a place where people traded stories. Bruce Hamilton, Lawrence Till Doty and many others loafed around at the barbershop. Melvin and Tiny Porter would come in and spend the afternoons every year watching

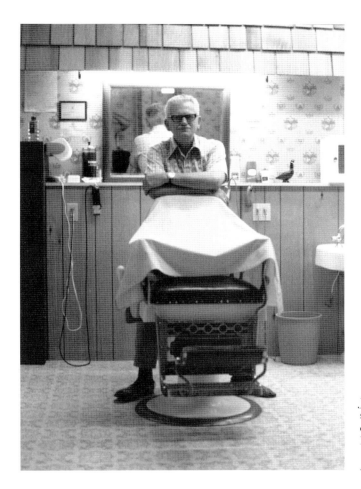

Jimmie Oldson standing behind his chair at Oldson's Barber Shop, circa 1960s. *Oldham County Historical Society*.

the World Series and drink Cokes. I had a Coke machine in there. Everybody would come to town on Saturday, and I would open at 8:00 a.m. They would be lined up. At one time, I had four barbers in there to help me on Saturdays. I would open at 8:00 a.m. and close at 9:00 p.m. For a shave, I would lean them back in the chair and work up a lather and put it on their face and wrap two hot towels over the lather. Then I would wash that off and lather them up again and start shaving. I had straight razors and leather straps, and you had to use the right strokes. When I started, haircuts were seventy-five cents and a shave was a quarter. I also had a shoeshine boy. Skeeter Taylor and Jack Durrett both worked for me at different times and shined shoes. Ballard Clark, Elliot Netherton and Mr. Wooldridge would bring their shoes down to get them shined during the week.

One Saturday, I was cutting hair at the shop. Sonny McHargue lived right behind me. Him and Tommy Ballard were young boys then and full of mischief. We were busy, the shop was full and there was no air conditioning. I had the chair next to the window. It was hot, and the window was open. Someone hit the window, and the window slammed shut. I put the window up and looked out but didn't see anybody. It happened again, and this time I saw Sonny and Tommy running around the corner. So, I had an old mop bucket, and I filled it with water to throw it out the window on them next time. Wasn't long and I could see a shadow coming around the corner, so I grabbed the bucket and threw out the water—but it wasn't the two boys. It was a farmer. He had a white shirt on and overalls, and boy was he mad. I don't blame him! He gave me a good cussing! I told him how sorry I was.

Just this past Sunday, there was a young man in church, Charlie Prather's grandson came up to me and said, "Jimmy, I had my picture taken with you for my first haircut." I have had two others here recently, one stopped me when I was mowing the grass and said, "How do you do?" and he said, "Jim Oldson, you don't remember me; I am Gordon McCombs, and you gave me my first haircut!" I had many, many of them. It was tough giving those first haircuts, and the mothers would usually bring them in. The little boys usually had long, curly hair, the mothers would cry—and it would break my heart too! The mothers would try to hold them and keep them calm. I used to give them a sucker, but they would get hair all over it. As soon as you turned the clipper on, they would start crying. The worst I remember was Tom Manby. I believe he was the loudest I ever heard; you could hear him beller all the way down the street! I have no idea how many I have given. I gave Don Bryant, Larry Bryant, Harry and Jean Brown's boy Greg—I could name them all day long.

The weirdest haircut was Dr. Walsh's boy, Ed. Ed came in the barbershop and wanted a Don Eagle cut. You give them a burr first and then peel them right down the back and bring it to a point; it's an Indian type of haircut. You see them more today.

THE LAGRANGE POST OFFICES

The building at 200 East Main was constructed as the first post office for the city of LaGrange circa 1914. Before that time, it occupied various storefronts and businesses. As the community grew during the 1970s, the post office moved to First Street, in a building now occupied by City Place, and then later to its present location. The following stories by mail carriers Noralee Moock and Herbie Hendron are just too good not to include.

Noralee Moock

I started working for the LaGrange Post Office in 1969. They put out notices around town that they needed help. Mr. Dawson (the postmaster) told me I couldn't have the job; a woman couldn't do it. So they put the notices out again, and this time I went to Louisville to take the civil service test and passed it. While there were three other men that qualified for the job, they didn't want it, so Mr. Dawson said, "Well, I guess I have to take you." He didn't think I could carry the bag walking around the street to deliver mail. You had to train on your own time, and you had to purchase your hat. They had no uniforms for women. I also wasn't allowed to wear pants, but they did let me wear pants in the winter when it got cold. I had to train with Roger Rankin, and he was the gentlest man you could ever meet, and people were unmerciful on him about having to train a woman. They told him I "was here to take his job." The second day I went out with Roger, Mr. Dawson told Roger that I would have to carry that bag all day long, and he said if I couldn't carry that bag, then I couldn't do the job.

The very next day was Saturday and the Reader's Digests *had come out. Everyone back then got a* Reader's Digest, *and they were so heavy in my pack. Well, I went down Second Street and then up that steep hill on Highway 53 to Washington Street. I thought to myself if I got up that hill I was going to quit, but when I got up the hill, I got my second wind. Then a big storm came out that afternoon, and it just poured on me, and I thought they are going to fire me because it made me a half hour late back to the office. Dutch Hargrove was at the office, and he said, "I can't believe you are back so soon; no one else is back yet!" It was an eight-mile walking route.*

Later, I was training to take Salty William's route, which went down to the Bottom [the African American section of town], *and the men down there started giving me a hard time. Betty Lou Shirley (who ran a business at the Bottom) came out, and boy did she get after those men. She told them to treat me with respect, and they did. She did a lot of nice things for the community.*

When I first started, a lot of people criticized me because they said I was taking a man's job, but I said, "No, the men that applied were offered the job and didn't want it." I had a lot of people that supported me too. Mr.

Dawson turned around too and supported me—particularly after I filled in for others when they went on vacation. I carried mail for six days for six weeks that first summer. Mr. Dawson called me in and said, "I owe you an apology and should not have denied you an application," and he said, "I really didn't think a woman could do the job."

Herbie Hendron
I had pretty much all of LaGrange when I started my post office route in LaGrange. I had a morning route and an afternoon route—all walking—about eight or nine miles. One thing I liked about working at the post office is that you were out walking and could get your mind off things. I didn't mind the weather. I used to check on people. I would take food to Jean Hancock when she was sick, and I would always shovel snow off the walk for Velma Jeffries. The only thing I ever had a problem with was snakes. One time I was walking with Bob Bohannon, who was the postmaster at the time, and he would check on my route. I came upon two snakes on the sidewalk, and I jumped and threw a block into him and laid him straight! He was sore about three days. And another time, I was at the trailer court, and some of the kids put a possum in the pickup box. It was in the summer, must have been one hundred degrees, and I opened that thing up and that thing, hair was standing up on its back and it hissed at me! I told that guy running the place, "get it out of there; I'm not picking no mail up until that thing is gone!"

When I first started delivering mail, I had two dogs, down near Adams Street, a black lab and another one, and they would meet me every day. Later, I had a big old St. Bernard, Mandy, that belonged to Phil and Bobby Ward. That dog would watch for me and go with me every day walking my routes, and she would follow me all the way down to the post office. I would put her in the truck and take her home. I had people say that even when I was sick, she would walk my routes by herself at the same time. She did that for years. That dog wouldn't let nothing bother me, no other dogs or anybody.

Ballard Brothers Store

The Ballard Brothers Store at 118 East Main Street was an important dry goods business that retained its basic purpose as a family department store as it changed ownership throughout the twentieth century. The Ballard Brothers business started in 1886 in an unidentified building on Main Street, and then the Ballard family built the large Ballard Brothers Store around 1910. In a store advertisement taken from the 1926 anniversary edition of the *Oldham Era*, they advertised the following merchandise:

> As the years have come, we have added new lines, thus keeping abreast of the times. On our shelves will be found new, up to date stock including the following famous lines: Dress Goods in the best silks and crepes, Phoenix Silk Hose, Hole proof Hosiery, Wilson Bros. Hosiery, Underwear, Shirts and ties, Musing's Underwear, Manchester Shirts, Tom Sawyer Shirts and Blouses, Porter Bros. and Young's Hats, Hansen's Dress Gloves and Work Gloves, Florsheim Shoes, Queen Quality Shoes, Red Goose Shoes, Big Moore Work Shirts, Carhart Overalls, Tiger Brand Overalls. In our grocery department we handle Ballard's Obelisk and Self-Rising Flour, Smithfield's Best, Eminence Leader and Lexington Cream Flour, Vissman's Derby Hams and Breakfast Bacon, Pure Lard and Picnic Hams. Our shelves are always full of the best lines of all kinds of canned goods. We know that we can satisfy your wants.

Ruby Duncan remembers the Ballard business when she was a child during the 1930s:

> The Ballard Brothers Store was on the corner of Main and Walnut Streets. I needed some money for something at school. Mother wrapped one dozen eggs in newspaper and put them in an oatmeal box and told me to take them to Ballard Brothers Store, that they bought fresh country eggs and I could have the money for what I needed at school. I did, and I received enough money for the event at school.

Sometime during the 1940s or early '50s, the store changed hands and was owned Edith Shearer, who had several business partners over the years, so it was first Wise and Shearers, Jones and Shearers and Brizidene and Shearers. They carried popular brands of clothing over those years, such as Grasshopper Shoes and Ship and Shore women's wear, along with men's dress and farm clothing, children's clothing and underwear. Sometime in the 1970s, it changed and became a Western Auto Store. Since that time, it has changed into many different venues.

Masonic Lodge, Fortitude Lodge No. 47

This building at 127 East Main Street has several interesting details that highlight its purpose as a Masonic lodge. The beautiful stained-glass window on the second floor embellishes the important symbols of the Masonic life. The cornerstone on the first floor by the sidewalk with the building's date (1911) demonstrates that this building was dedicated and received the Masonic rites. Freemasons in their ceremonies have made the cornerstone a symbol of the individual Mason and the sacrifices of labor and time necessary to build a moral and Masonic edifice. The cornerstones are usually hollow and contain small objects like coins, photographs and Masonic tools like trowels.

The cornerstone also symbolizes sturdiness, morality and truth. It is customary for Masons to lay the cornerstones of public buildings through ceremony—traditionally with the stone placed in the northeast corner of the foundation. Physical cornerstones used in ceremonies in which Masons are erecting buildings traditionally show the date, the name of the Grand Lodge, the grand master and the Masonic emblem. Cornerstones have been part of the construction or dedication of many federal buildings and seats of state government since the beginnings of our country. Benjamin Franklin, while grand master of Pennsylvania, established the tradition beginning with the cornerstone-laying of the state house in Philadelphia, and George Washington laid the cornerstone of the Capitol building.

Fortitude Lodge No. 47 began with a charter from the Masons of Transylvania on September 1, 1818, by the Grand Lodge of Kentucky. The lodge was not very active until the 1840s, holding its meetings first in a small building that it shared with the LaGrange Christian Church on Jefferson Street and then for many years at the Funk Seminary, which became the Kentucky Masonic College. After the Masonic College closed and became the LaGrange Funk Seminary Elementary and High School, the lodge purchased the old Baptist church on Washington Street until 1910, when it built the current Masonic temple on the corner of Main and Cedar Streets. There is a dedicated cornerstone on the building's northeast side at the intersection of Walnut and Main Streets that is easily viewed by the sidewalk corner. The lodge still owns this building and rents store space on the first floor. The Order of the Eastern Star, local chapter Rob Morris No. 114, organized in 1909, shares meeting space with Fortitude Lodge.

Samuel DeHaven, in his "Remembrance" taken from the *Oldham Era*, recalled the site was first occupied by the Graingers Company:

The first store building of much size and consequence was erected by the "Graingers" Company. The "Graingers" was a sort of politico-farmer organizations, akin to the populist, and very strong in the West. They put up the building on the present site of the Masonic Temple. Here they had a big store supposed to be patronized by all farmers. Jim Settle had the contract to dig the cellar and I worked for him after school hours. He and I alone dug that cellar.

The first floor of the Masonic lodge has always served as a retail building of some sort. Pool halls, teen clubs, bookstores and antique malls have all occupied the first-floor space over the decades, but the second floor still functions as the home for Fortitude Lodge 47 and OES Rob Morris No. 114.

J.R. Gatewood's Drugstore

J.R. "Rush" Gatewood owned this store at 125 East Main Street (circa 1911) through the mid-twentieth century. He sold liquor from the back room of the store, and there was a regular group of local businessmen who would play pinochle in the back room. Dot Smith worked for Gatewood and recalled her experiences at the drugstore:

While living on Woodlawn, I received a call from Martha Ireland asking if I would like to come work at Gatewood Drugstore. The kids were in school, so I worked there for several years. When I worked for Gatewood Drugstore, I remember Dr. Stearns (the veterinarian) coming in to get his penicillin tablets and such for his patients (dogs, cats, etc.). When my kids were sick, Mr. Ireland (the pharmacist at Gatewood's) would always give me the penicillin tablets that Dr. Stearns used for his patients because Mr. Ireland said "they were a little stronger," they were cheaper and they worked!

Mr. Gatewood was so nice, and every time there was a train that went by, he would step outside and count the cars. He would say, "Today there was sixty-seven cars" or "Today there was one hundred." Mr. Gatewood lived on Kentucky Street next to the Nethertons. He lived there for years.

Mr. Gatewood took care of many, many people. I don't know how many kids he sent to college, but a lot, he would pay their tuition. He paid for people's surgeries if they couldn't afford them. People would come in and tell Mr. Gatewood if someone had a problem, then he would take care of them. Mr. Gatewood asked us never to tell anyone that he helped people in the community. He loved horse races and always went to the Derby.

D.W. Griffith Theatre

There are many wonderful recollections that people have about the D.W. Griffith Theatre at 123 Main Street. It was central for entertainment for families and particularly kids, who could spend a Saturday afternoon for small change. In the early years, westerns were popular feature films, replaced by thrillers, horror movies and second-run feature films during the 1950s. I remember going with my brother, Joe, to see *The Blob*, which was a scary movie and gave me vivid nightmares. Richard Reynolds recalled when the theater was segregated: "We went to the D.W. Griffith Theatre, but they made us [Black kids] go upstairs, through the projection room and sit in a space about ten by twelve feet. We threw popcorn at the kids below."

D.W. Griffith Theatre at 123 East Main provided cheap entertainment for kids on Saturdays while parents shopped during the 1930s through '50s. Arson was suspected for its demise in 1960. *Oldham County Historical Society.*

The D.W. Griffith Theatre opened sometime during the late 1930s and was destroyed by fire on January 17, 1960. A large portion of the building burned, but some details of the façade survived, and the building has been renovated and served as many businesses over the years. Johnnie Glauber served on the fire department and remembers when the building burned:

> *At the time the D.W. Griffith fire happened on Main Street, I went around the corner on Main Street, and flames were coming out the marquee and going up the second floor. That fire was set. South Oldham, Middletown, Ballardsville and a crew from Lyndon were all called in to the fire. I met a chief from Lyndon, Buz Pearce, who later became my mentor. LaGrange buildings are structured where the rafters go through the walls into other buildings. There was the theater, jewelry store and Cassady Insurance beside the theater. The Lyndon crew went into the jewelry store and began pulling the ceilings and opened it up. When the theater blew up, it blew the roof off Gatewood Drugstore, a few stores down, which set back down about a foot off!*

The Central Hotel

The Central Hotel at 114 East Main Street is one of the most prominent buildings on Main Street, with its cast-iron storefront and its slate roof that spells out "Hotel." The history of the building site is predated by one of the original pre–Civil War hotels in LaGrange that succumbed to fire at the turn of the twentieth century. The building had many uses throughout the twentieth century, including a funeral home, post office, harness shop, law offices, specialty shops and tearoom. Most recently, the old hotel has been on a series of ghost tours sponsored by Discover Main Street LaGrange. The western section of the of the building housed a post office in 1908.

During its funeral home years, the Peak Funeral Home (and later Peak-Adkins Funeral Home) handled the arrangement for D.W. Griffith's funeral when he was interred at the Mount Tabor Cemetery in Centerfield in 1948. Internationally known as the "Father of Modern Film," Griffith came from a family that dates back to the county's early history. A special funeral service was held for Griffith at the Hollywood Masonic Temple before his body came back to his humble beginnings in Oldham County for burial. Reverend Lloyd Moody, minister of the LaGrange Methodist Church, said the final

Central Hotel (circa 1905) has served as a hotel, post office, saddlery shop and funeral home over the years. It is a popular site for ghost tours. *Harris Collection, Oldham County Historical Society.*

rites. The cemetery is located by the Mount Tabor Methodist Church that Griffith attended as a youth. His family farm is nearby.

The original hotel located on the site dated back to the 1850s and was once owned by Emily Waide (1823–1909) with her husband, William Meriwether Waide (b. 1820). They moved to LaGrange to open a hotel shortly after the railroad was built through town in the 1850s. They moved with their five daughters, Sarah Ann, Emily Nevel (nicknamed Johnnie after Emily's brother), Mary Elizabeth (Cora) and Eliza Todd and Francis Givens. Emily's younger brother and sister, Gus and Sallie, as well as her mother also moved to LaGrange and lived with Emily's family. One of their daughters, Virginia "Jennie" Adelaide, died from typhoid fever before their move from the hotel that burned down. The Waide House Hotel was originally located on the site of the Ballard Brothers Store. After a fire burned the building, the Waide family took over a second hotel, where the Central Hotel stands today. According to an article by Frank L. Crafft, "Passenger trains stopped in front of the Waide House, in which was the ticket office and waiting room."

The following stories about the Central Hotel are taken from a transcript in the archives of the Oldham County History Center from an interview of Emily Waide conducted by her granddaughter Amanthus Kimball (1871–1959). I have used Emily's stories many times on tours and featured them in various articles because she so succinctly describes life in LaGrange during the Civil War:

> *One morning as I was in the kitchen making biscuits, Gus came in and said, "Sister I have enlisted in the army and am going to fight for my country." I knew Mr. Waide could not go, as he was in poor health and my boys were not old enough, but Gus was as my own child, and my heart ached when he told me, although I admired his spirit. All of my spare time was spent in preparing for his departure, and the day the news came for his company to march, there were many sad hearts besides mine. It had been arranged that all friends and relatives of the members of the company should meet at the fairgrounds several miles from LaGrange to bid farewell to our boys in blue, and a big dinner was prepared. Everyone who came brought baskets of the best they had to eat and all enjoyed our last meal together, but enjoyed it with aching hearts, for there would be some of those brave boys who would never return.*
>
> *At three o'clock, the bugle sounded, the company formed in line shouldered their guns, and amid goodbyes and good wishes, with much weeping and many heartaches, they marched off to take part in that deadliest of wars. We who were not able to go, and were left behind, determined to do our part, and we had many opportunities. Trains began to pass through our little town, many times a day, filled with first the Blues and then the Grays, but all bound for the same place. They had to be fed, and our tables were filled most of the time. We prepared baskets of good things to eat, bundles of bandages, clothes and medicine, and our girls met each train—gave what they had to the soldiers and received many a grateful smile and sometimes a handkerchief bearing the owner's name, a little flag or some token which the soldiers might have and drop to them from the car window.*
>
> *As the weeks and months passed, reports came constantly only of an increase in the terrible trouble. There seemed no end to it, and the dead and dying were daily brought in. We heard once in a while from Gus. He had been in many battles and narrowly escaped. In one letter he wrote, "my hat is full of bullet holes, but as yet I am unhurt."*
>
> *We kept two large handsome flags hanging in the front of the hotel, one of them belonging to my daughter Sallie, who, with her sister Johnnie, was*

full of patriotism. Mr. Waide, though a strong Union man, was kind to the Rebel soldiers, and never did we receive unkind treatment from them. Our house was often used to hide property belonging to the Union army. One day, the Rebels were heard marching into town. Johnnie ran for the handsome flag, took it to the garden and buried it. By that time, one of the soldiers was at the house and said they had heard that we owned a very handsome flag, which they wanted. Sallie said, "We have one, but it is my own property, and you will not get it." He said he would report to the captain, and in a little while the captain came, asked for Mr. Waide and wanted to know if we could feed fifty Rebel soldiers. Mr. Waide said, "Yes, I can, and if you demand it, I will."

They of course demanded it, and my girls and I with the help of my servants went to work, and we did give them a good meal. While we were preparing their food, they said to Mr. Waide, "We want the three hundred guns and blankets belonging to the Union army that have been stored here." Fortunately, we had sent them to Louisville the night before. They did not believe it and ordered the house searched. The captain was told that he might search under one condition: that he and one of his men accompany Mr. Waide, and neither his daughters' or my room be entered. The captain had heard of several kind acts we had done his side of the army and not only agreed to the condition but said they would not interfere in regard to the flag either, saying, "You have fed us so bountifully and have been so honest with us, we will only thank you and bid you goodbye."

And such were many of the experiences we had during the war, always receiving kindness where kindness was given. One night, a poor forlorn fellow in rags came to our door. It was a freezing cold night, and that bedraggled Rebel asked if he and some of his comrades might sleep in our stable. We were afraid for them to occupy the stable as we, having had so many experiences with fire, were afraid to run the risk of having them stay there and probably smoke, so we offered them our long dining room which had a stove in it, and told them they could sleep on the floor on comforts which we would furnish them. Little Sose, child-like, was peeping around the corner and heard some of their conversation. He came running to me and said, "Mama, those men are hungry. I heard one of them say, 'I believe if we would ask these people, they would give us something to eat.'"

I told the girls, and all of them went to work, and in half an hour they were the happiest soldiers you could think of—hot coffee, sandwiches, eggs and pies were passed around, and nothing was left but empty dishes.

> *With all of their experiences with the Rebels, my girls were true to their cause, the "Union forever." When the trains would stop in front of the hotel, we often took little Florence out front and stood her on a table and let her sing for the soldiers. She liked nothing better, and the soldiers were greatly pleased and amused, for she was not much more than a baby and could sing unusually well.*

Gus lived on to raise a family of his own. Emily and her husband sold the hotel sometime in 1867 or early '68 and moved to Louisville, and shortly thereafter, in 1868, Emily's husband died. In 1869, Emily's first grandchild was born, and she spent her future years tending to her family, grandchildren and great-grandchildren, visiting different places where they lived until her death in 1909.

Kroger

There were several grocery stores on Main Street during the twentieth century, and the Kroger Store at 110–12 East Main Street was one of the largest. The side-by-side central entrances made it a convenient entrance and exit for customers. Jimmy Roberts fondly remembered working there during his teen years:

> *When I worked at Kroger's, we had to put the produce up every night when we closed at six o'clock. We put the produce in large wooden barrels, with dampened burlap bags put over it, layering between the onions, and so on, building up, then chunks of ice over that. The trucks would deliver their groceries every night. They would back up at the front door of the store to unload and jackknife the cab of the truck so it was alongside the railroad track because the trains would still be running through the night. We would go in the next morning before school to put the produce back on the shelves. Bobby Burge, John Madden, my brother worked there for a while. Bobby was the meat cutter. We also carried groceries out for the customers. The manager would also lock us in the store at night at six and also stock the shelves when a truck wasn't coming. He would come back and unlock around seven and look to see what we had done and let us out. As soon as he locked that door, Bobby Burge would holler, "Let's go, gang," and we would have bologna sandwiches, a twenty-nine-cent bag of potato chips and everybody would get*

one of those small Cokes out of the meat cooler. We ate our sandwiches in about five minutes and then went back to stocking the shelves. I ran into the store manager, Paul Kramer, many years later, and I said, "Boy, in today's world if the government found out you locked us in the store…" He laughed and said, "I would have been hung from a tall tree on a short rope." He said, "What did you all do when I left the store?" I said, "We had a bologna sandwich and a Coke and went to work." He said, "You know, you won't believe this, but we did the same thing when I was a kid. I figured it was happening but wasn't anything I was going to fuss about."

Glauber's Five and Ten Cent Store

This business is part of a two-story, four-unit brick building that has served LaGrange over the past one hundred years as many different businesses with addresses 115–21 East Main. Businesses over the years include Mary Dee's Sweet Shop, Sadie's Restaurant, Barr's Grocery and Glauber's, as well as the more recent Old Oak Frame House, Irish Rover Too and Ernesto's.

Glauber's Five and Ten Cent Store was one of my childhood favorites. It was the store I could afford as a child! I could buy all my Christmas gifts for my parents, grandparents and favorite people. They had beautiful hand-embroidered handkerchiefs for both men and women packaged neatly in a box with a cellophane window tied with a bow. I could buy a surprise ball for a nickel, which was a crepe paper ball that, when unwrapped, had small toys snugly intertwined all the way to the end. During the Easter season, they sold live baby chicks that had been dyed blue, green and pink; those that I brought home turned out to be roosters! Johnny Glauber provided a wonderful story about his family store that I recorded for our Living Treasures Oral History Program:

I was born on June 3, 1938, on Main Street (in LaGrange) above our store, which was Glauber's Five and Ten Cent Store. My dad's name was John William Glauber, and my mother was Opal Stapp Glauber. My dad was from Harrodsburg, and my mom was from Russell Springs. They were married in Campbellsville, Kentucky, in 1932. My dad was working in Campbellsville at the time in one of the groceries, and he found out there was a business for sale in LaGrange in 1933. He came up here and liked what he saw, and Mom and Dad moved in above the store in the apartment.

Glauber's Five and Ten Cent Store was a popular variety store. *Oldham County Historical Society.*

    I was born there, and we lived there until I was two and then moved on Highway 146 across from the parsonage of Baptist DeHaven Memorial Church. While we lived there, Mom and Dad built their home on Fourth Street, where my sister still lives. My sister is ten years younger than me.

    The Five and Ten Cent Store was right in the middle of the block. On one side was Barr's Grocery, and the other was Mary Dee's Sweet Shop. I remember, especially on Friday and Saturday nights, people gathering in the back of the store, by the pot-bellied stove. There would be twelve or fifteen people just sitting around the stove, talking and enjoying each other's company. Every evening, my job was to go to the back door to the coal shed and bring in the coal for the stove. Back then there were steam engine trains that came through town, and all the ash from the smoke would settle on the sidewalks. Another job I had was to sweep the sidewalks every morning. When I got older, I helped Dad wash the windows and decorate the store windows.

    I remember the Pan American passenger train came through from Chicago, I believe. People would wave, and I would sit out on the curb. I really enjoyed the Derby trains. They would hook on these elaborate cars on the back of the regular passenger trains with people going to the Derby. You would see them going back from the Derby on Mondays!

    They didn't close the stores until nine on Friday and Saturday nights. On those nights, you could hardly walk on Main Street because of the crowds of people—it was so crowded! Cars would be parked up on Jefferson Street and between Third and Fourth Streets; it was busy.

Dad had a dry goods store and had everything from women's hair barrettes, kids' toys, a small selection of hardware and they built a balcony and put a shoe department up there.

Christmastime was very good for me. My dad and mom gave me a lot of toys. They were metal toys: airplanes, fire trucks, the old Mattel toys. He had five and dime type toys too. For Easter, he had stuffed bunny rabbits, egg dyes, things like that. We had a good candy part too—Mom ran that. It was on the right aisle under the stairway. It was fifteen feet long. They had bulk candy, chocolate drops, hard candies. And the other part they had candy bars. I remember one time my dad ran low in candy; he got his candy from Axton Candy Company. Dad got hold of Mr. Abbott of Abbott Transfer Company, and Mr. Abbott went down to Louisville and got it for him. The candy came in ten- and fifteen-pound bags.

When the Mary Dee Sweet Shop closed, Mom and Dad bought it and started a restaurant by the ten-cent store. We had breakfast, lunch and dinner at our restaurant. The dinner consisted of meat and two sides. It was just regular short-order sandwiches for lunch and typical breakfast. Ada Lee (Mr. Tommy Lee's wife) and her sister were the cooks. The waitresses were Mrs. Montgomery, Mrs. Button, Mrs. Ballard and Mrs. Horine and, of course, Mom. They also served Rotary Club each week.

Mrs. Lee would be back there cooking in the summer, and there was no air conditioner, there were just exhaust fans. She would just be singing, and she wore a bandanna on her head. She would catch me sneakin' a taste of potato salad; she would chase me out the back door and tell me she would tell my daddy. Dad was called Big John, and I was always called Little Johnny. There are still people around that call me Little Johnny. On a Friday night, Mom would fix fried shrimp and frog leg dinners. One night, she had homemade chop suey, and everyone just ate it up. I think she was the first one in town to have it.

McDowell Pharmacy and Head's Drugstore

In 1868, W.A. McDowell and his family started a pharmacy in LaGrange that became a familiar establishment cherished by the community for years to come. The first store burned to the ground. The McDowells lived on the second floor of the building and barely escaped. The McDowells rebuilt their store, directly across the street from the old building at 104–08 East Main, where it remains today. Reuben "Bookie" Taylor recalled the store's early years in "Remembrances of Things Past":

> *I always remember the McDowell's Drug Store. It was a real pharmacy, where prescriptions were compounded. There were few proprietary medicines, except Lydia Pinkham's Vegetable Compound or Wine of Cordue or Wintersmith's Chill Tonic—whose popularity, I was told, was largely due to their high percentage of alcohol. Those were the days of quinine and calomel an—get this—laudanum (cocaine), which you could get without a prescription. Mighty good for toothache or whatever ailed you. McDowell's had the first telephone. It was such a comfort to be able to run to the phone and twist the crank and say, "Maud, quick, call the neighbors. Our chimney is on fire!"*

With the addition of a soda fountain, McDowell's became a very popular destination. All of the syrups and carbonated water were manufactured in special equipment that McDowell installed in the drugstore.

> *To begin the foundation of the business 2,000 gallons of carbonated water was used; to sweeten the water 600 gallons of syrup, made at home by the firm, was consumed; 8 barrels of sugar was required to make the syrup; ice cream, to give the beverage that touch of excellence so loved by Johnnie and his best girlfriend, was used to the tune of 500 gallons; 20,000 straws were got away with and nobody knows how much ice.*

Charles Davis bought the drugstore business in the early twentieth century and continued through World War II until Billy Head purchased the business, under whom it continued to operate through the late 1970s. He was a quiet man, always with a smile, and served the community with many fond memories from his customers and employees. Barbara Hoffman Head probably worked at Head's Drugstore the longest. The following are her recollections:

> *When I started working at Head's, we had soda tables and the old-fashioned fountain that seated about five people. We had a big mirror in the back of it, which we always decorated for different occasions. You could get an ice cream cone for a nickel or a double for a dime. You could also get a nickel*

Druggist Billy Head fills prescriptions at Head's Drugstore. *Oldham County Historical Society.*

cherry Coke. I had a lady over on 42, and every time she would come to town, she had to have her ten-cent cherry Coke. We had chocolate, vanilla, strawberry, fudge royal and sometimes a seasonal ice cream. The ice cream came from Sealtest in Louisville in three- to five-gallon containers. Back then, you had to stay in the store to eat your ice cream and drink your Coke because we didn't have "to go" cups back then. I would take the containers home and make things out of them like sewing other things.

We didn't have sandwiches. You could get a soda, a milkshake, a sundae, a banana split. And we had a freezer that we carried half gallons of ice cream, and people would come by after church and get them a half gallon to take home for Sunday dinner. We had that freezer that you could slide open. We had the candy rack, cigar rack, big jewelry counter and big, tall ceilings, and on the wall were cabinets and shelves that you had to get a ladder to get to the top to restock.

When I was a kid, the first drugstore I remember was Davis's Drugstore, where Dizzy Dave's is now. That is where I went as a kid, the few times we would get to go. They had the tall booths and the fountain you could stand up to. Doc Davis, Charles Davis, had a daughter named Barbara and had a son, whose name I can't think of. Doc Davis sold out to Mr. Head. Mr. Head was in World War II and was stationed in Alaska.

Mr. Head was more than a druggist. He had so much training that he could tell a family almost as much as what a doctor could tell them. And I think families would try to save their money on doctor's bills and go talk to Mr. Head. He issued credit to a lot of these farmers that had tobacco crops; at the end of that year, they would come in and pay off their bill for the whole year. Their charges were monthly. Everything had to be written down; no computers back then! You stood there in a notebook, wrote down the person's name, exactly what they bought, how much it was and the secretary sent out the bills each month.

I never will forget we had this little old lady from Westport. She would come in and pay her bill, then she would come up front and get a box of chewing tobacco. "Now you put it in two sacks, Barbara!" She didn't want the people who brought her to town to know that she chewed tobacco! I had another little lady would come in and get her corncob pipe.

Lots of people would come in and get their stomach medicine, and it didn't seem like we sold a lot of aspirin and headache pills that people use today. One thing at Christmas, the counter right in front of the fountain was always clear, and we would decorate it with Bibles. Some of the nicest Bibles you could find, and we would put a little Christmas tree in the middle. We sold more Bibles at Christmastime. We would go to the old Belknap Hardware Store in July (in downtown Louisville) and go Christmas shopping for items to sell in the store. Jean Hall and I would go pick out the things. I worked forty-five hours one week and forty-eight the next; I worked every other Sunday, and we had one afternoon a week off. Saturday we were open from 8:00 a.m. until 10:00 p.m. The rest of the week we were open from 8:00 a.m. until 9:00 p.m., and we had an hour for lunch.

We had a hot nut case that was between the candy and tobacco. It was always in front of the window. There were times I would be putting candy in the case, and Dr. Walsh would come in and run his finger down my back and make me jump. Dr. Walsh was the family doctor, and of course, we had Dr. Blaydes, and back then you didn't see a doctor unless it was really necessary. I fell off the greenhouse one time, and both the doctors were out of town. We had an old coal mining doctor whose office was over Rosenburg's Department Store; he was from the coal country in East Kentucky. So I went to see him, and he didn't have any anesthetic to freeze the foot, so he sent Daddy to Mallory Taylor to get some antiseptic, and Daddy held my foot down while the doctor sewed it up.

Flo Thomas Lewis recalls an interesting moment at Head's during the segregation years:

> *When I was about twelve, Momma would let me and my best friend, Jewell Johnson, walk up to LaGrange. Momma would call "Dr. Billy Head" at Head's Drugstore to get medicine, and we'd pick it up. We would walk into Head's Drugstore and get a nickel and buy a cherry Coke, and he would say, "There are Ann and Christina's girls." So we would take our Cokes and sit on the step on the street. One day, we went in and got our cherry Cokes and decided to sit on the stool in the store. Mr. Head said, "Girls, you are not supposed to be sitting there, you need to go outside and drink your Cokes." Jewell turned to me and said, "We are not going outside to drink the Cokes." So we left the Cokes and went through the store, and there was a magazine stand with* True Story *magazines, and we took the magazines and walked out. We walked on down to the depot, and we sat down and started reading this* True Story. *Jewell looked at me and said, "Flo, do you think Mr. Head knows we took these books?" and I said, "No." And she said if he did, he will tell our mommas and daddies, so we turned around and took the books back in the store and put them up. And our Cokes were still sitting there, and we walked over and got the Cokes and went out and sat down on the street. I will never forget that because our conscience told us to go back!*

T.W. Duncan Hardware Store

This keystone building at 101 East Main Street sits at an important business intersection of LaGrange and sets the tone, along with the 101 West Building, for Main Street businesses. Its earliest proprietor was Lindsey Duncan, who operated the store as a butcher shop sometime before 1912. Lindsey and his brother, Richard O. Duncan, operated the store as Duncan and Company and sold general merchandise. The store was used as a hardware store and went under the name of Brazin Hardware in the late 1930s and early '40s.

The large room in the rear of the building upstairs was used as a winter croquet club in 1938. According to Bobby Hampton, "I was eleven years old, and all the other players were grown men, but I was pretty good. In fact, I was better than all of them except one man. We would put sawdust

The Duncan Hardware Store at 101 East Main (circa 1900), later replaced as Jerry's Corner Store through the 1980s. *Left to right*: Raymond Cunningham, T.N. Roberts and E.M. Bland. *Oldham County Historical Society.*

on the floor and drill holes in the floor to put the wickets in. In the '30s and '40s, Dr. W.H. Cox ran a dental office in the front part of the upstairs." J.W. Hall was one of Dr. Cox's patients and remembers his experience: "Dr. Cox was my dentist. He had an old pedal drill he ran with his foot, and every once in a while, the drill would get stuck in your tooth, and he would let out a few cuss words and he would get up and go behind the curtain and have a drink. Sometimes, if you had to have a tooth pulled, he would send you up to Dr. McGregor."

Jerry Meers moved to LaGrange in 1943 and opened Jerry's Corner Store selling hardware, housewares, furniture, appliances, Firestone tires, toys and sporting goods. Riva Morgan, who worked at Jerry's for thirty-eight years, said, "At Christmastime, we sold a lot of toys. It was fun to unwrap all the pretty dolls. It was like Christmas every time we received a new shipment of merchandise. I enjoyed unpacking all of those boxes."

In 1990, Jerry's Corner Store closed, and there was a public auction. The building has since housed several businesses.

The Bank of Oldham County

There were several banks that began on Main Street. In 1873, the General Assembly passed an act to incorporate the People's Bank, which was a wood-frame building on the north corner of Main and First Streets. In May 1884, the Oldham Bank was organized with capital stock of $100,000 and began business with $30,000 paid in. The first directory comprised S.E. DeHaven, J.H. Vivian, D.H. French, P.S. Head, J.F. Buckner, Zack Head, J.E. Vincent, Thomas Duncan and Chas. S. Fible. The bank locations shifted around Main Street over several years. Oldham Bank (circa 1904) was located at 101 West Main and First Street. With its stunning detailed cornices and sign plate, it remains as an important anchor for Main Street. Its first location was at 117 West Main, which dates back to 1840 and is one of the oldest remaining structures on Main Street.

The People's Bank was replaced by the two-story brick building that became the Bank of Oldham County and remained as such for many decades. The two-story brick structure flanked by Doric columns and three-bay main façade trimmed in cast stone is typical of early twentieth-century commercial styling, according to the National Register of Historic Places. The bank built and moved into a new building at the corner of First and Jefferson Streets in the 1970s (now the Fiscal Court Building).

Banking before credit cards was a different world than today; loans were very personal, and contact was face to face with the bank president and loan officers. It was all local. Children were encouraged to have their own personal savings accounts with the bank in those years. I remember walking up many times to the teller at the Bank of Oldham County to deposit my nickels and dimes in my savings account. The following stories from Flo Thomas Lewis and Dot Smith take us back to those simpler times.

Flo Thomas Lewis

I wanted education because when I was growing up, there was not really any jobs. I didn't want to work on a farm. I graduated from Lincoln Institute in May 1959, and I had an uncle who talked to Momma and Daddy and wanted to send me somewhere away to school. My momma said, "She doesn't need to be going anywhere." And my grandmamma said, "If Sissy wants to go, let her go." So in June of that year, I went down to the Western Kentucky Vocational School in Paducah and took up business classes. I went there two years, graduated and took the state test and was one of the highest on the typing scores. Alden's in Chicago came down to the vocational school and recruited some of us to go up there to work. They had a place for us to stay, the YMCA on 826 South Wabash and they started you out at ninety-six cents an hour.

I went home after I graduated and told my family I wanted to go to Chicago. And my grandmamma said I should go, and she would talk to my parents. So, then I talked to Momma and Daddy, and they said okay. Daddy said that I needed some money to take with me. So, my momma took me up to the bank, and we saw Mr. Sleadd, who was working at the bank and sitting outside the office [where you went to ask to borrow money]. *Mr. Sleadd asked Momma what she wanted, and she said that I graduated from school and I needed money to go to Chicago to be a clerk. Momma said I was going to be making ninety-six cents an hour. So she went inside the office to ask for money, and I sat across from Mr. Sleadd and waited for Momma to come out of the office. When she came out, Mr. Sleadd asked if they gave her the money. She said no, that we would have to borrow it against a car or something. Mr. Sleadd asked how much did she want, and she said, "I asked for $200 but said I would take $150," and Mr. Sleadd reached in his pocket and gave Mamma the $200. He said, "Now Anne, pay it when you can," and she said, "Okay."*

We walked out, and Momma took me and bought a three-piece suitcase. Before we left, my grandmamma said, "Now Sissy, how much you be making?" and I said, "Ninety-six cents an hour." And she said, "Now Sissy, how much do you love yourself?" and I said, "What?" And she said, "How much you think about yourself?" and I said, "A lot, I love myself a lot." And she said, "When you get your first check, you pay yourself. Pay yourself. If you make twenty dollars, give yourself a quarter. If you think a quarter is too much, give yourself ten cents. Always pay yourself. You always are paying everybody else, and you don't love everybody else, but you love yourself, so pay yourself."

Dot Smith

Later, I worked for the Bank of Oldham County, Citizen's Bank and then PNC for a total of twenty-one years, retiring in 1988. Dee Kelley asked to me to apply, and I did. It was the year I was forty years old, and Joe Pat and I moved in the house on Highway 146 (close to the fairgrounds). When I started with the Bank of Oldham County, it was located on the corner of First and Main in LaGrange. Banks were smaller then, and you had more direct contact with people who came in; it was more family oriented. If you wanted to borrow money back then, you didn't have to go through all that paperwork. When you walked in, if Mr. Sleadd knew you, you got your money. Mr. Taylor was also a wonderful man. There were no credit cards; you borrowed what you needed. There was very little interest, and you usually took money out on a short term, like three or six months. There was a little old man, Mr. Harris, made the best wine you ever tasted. At work, we would all save our empty salad dressing bottles, and he would fill up our bottles every year.

The Saurer Building and Kincaid Hardware Store

Casper Saurer and his son Charles constructed this building at 111 West Main Street. It is a Victorian commercial-style building that has always had a large store on the first floor with an "opry" house on the second floor, which served for many important cultural functions in LaGrange in the late nineteenth to early twentieth century. The Saurers burned the bricks for the building.

As a cultural center, it served as a movie theater, showing the very short feature silent films such as *The Great Train Robbery* before D.W. Griffith produced his epic *Birth of a Nation* in 1915. Students from the Funk Seminary High School held their graduation ceremonies here, and there were traveling shows and musicals, dances and parties that were held in this "opry hall." There was even a short basketball court where both girls and boys from LaGrange High School competed with other local schools.

Generally, the first floor was always a hardware and merchandise store until recently. The Saurer brothers offered farm goods and fertilizers, a men's clothing department, wallpaper and homeware, as well as axes, hatchets, carpenter's tools, nails, screws, fencing wires, iron roofing, paint and many other items along this line.

In the last part of the twentieth century, the Kincaid family owned the business and specialized in the last of the great hardware stores, where you could purchase just one nail or screw for that missing part on your farm machinery or house item. They took time with their customers to help find what they needed. Jim and Christie Kincaid Kamer were the last family members to own the store, which closed around 2001. Since that time, the store has served different businesses.

Bibliography

American Association of Meat Processors. March 19, 2022. www.aamp.com/aamp-history.
Applegate, Marjorie Morgan. "The Living Treasures Program." By Nancy S. Theiss. *Oldham Era*, September 18, 2008, B1.
Arvin, Bob. "The Living Treasurers Program." By Nancy S. Theiss. *Oldham Era*, June 19, 2014, B1.
Barnett, Barney. "The Living Treasures Program." By Nancy S. Theiss. *Oldham Era*, August 12, 2012, B1.
Beaumont, Diane. "The Living Treasures Program." By Nancy S. Theiss. *Oldham Era*, October 11, 2007, B1.
Booker, Diane. "The Living Treasures Program." By Nancy S. Theiss. *Oldham Era*, November 24, 2011, A11.
Booker, Harry. "The Living Treasures Program." By Nancy S. Theiss. *Oldham Era*, September 10, 2009, B1.
Brown, Bobby. "The Living Treasures Program." By Nancy S. Theiss. *Oldham Era*, April 19, 2018, B2.
Clarion (LaGrange, KY). "LaGrange Training School and Vicinity News." May 1925.
Clark, Billie. "The Living Treasures Program." By Nancy S. Theiss. *Oldham Era*, November 10, 2011, B1.
Clifford, Brad. "The Living Treasures Program." By Nancy S. Theiss. *Oldham Era*, March 20, 2014, B1.
Crafft, Frank L. "Reminiscences." *Oldham County Index*, August 12, 1901.
Duncan, Ruby. "The Living Treasures Program." By Nancy S. Theiss. *Oldham Era*, March 26, 2009, B1.
The Emprise Yearbook. Funk Seminary, 1921.
Glauber, Johnny. "The Living Treasures Program." By Nancy S. Theiss. *Oldham Era*, March 15, 2012, B1.
Green, Cindy. "The Living Treasures Program." By Nancy S. Theiss. *Oldham Era*, November 21, 2013, B1.

Bibliography

Hall, J.W., Jr. "The Living Treasures Program." By Nancy S. Theiss. *Oldham Era*, October 29, 2009, B1.

Hendron, Herbert. "The Living Treasures Program." By Nancy S. Theiss. *Oldham Era*, February 20, 2014, B1.

Henson, Ernie. "The Living Treasures Program." By Nancy S. Theiss. *Oldham Era*, November 26, 2015, B1.

Johnson, Emma Laura. "The Living Treasures Program." By Nancy S. Theiss. *Oldham Era*, June 26, 2008, B1.

Jones, Vivian Wright. "The Living Treasures Program." By Nancy S. Theiss. *Oldham Era*, March 9, 2020, B1.

"Kentucky State Census Report for Oldham County Schools, District B, 1900–1901." Frankfort, KY.

Kimbal, Amanthus. "Interview of Emily Waide." Oldham County History Center Archives, LaGrange, KY. 1909.

King and Head Pub. "A Good Hotel." *Oldham County Index*, August 22, 1890.

Klingenfus, Al. "The Living Treasures Program." By Nancy S. Theiss. *Oldham Era*, October 16, 2008, B1.

Kynett Church Deed. Archival Records, J.C. Barnett Library & Archives, Oldham County History Center, LaGrange, KY. April 7, 1868.

LaGrange Christian Church. "The Centennial of the LaGrange Christian Church 1845–1945." n.d.

The LaGrange Cookbook. Missionary Society of the Methodist Episcopal Church, LaGrange, KY. July 1913.

Lewis, Flo Thomas. "The Living Treasures Program." By Nancy S. Theiss. *Oldham Era*, June 9, 2011, B1.

Marrs, Reverend Elijah P. *Life and History of Rev. Elijah P. Marrs*. Louisville, KY: Beargrass Baptist Church, 1885. Repr., 1979.

McCombs, Beverly. "The Living Treasures Program." By Nancy S. Theiss. *Oldham Era*, May 16, 2013, B1.

Monroe, David. "The Living Treasures Program." By Nancy S. Theiss. *Oldham Era*, August 21, 2008, B1.

Moock, Noralee. "The Living Treasures Program." By Nancy S. Theiss. *Oldham Era*, December 18, 2014, B1.

Moore, Wendall. "The Living Treasures Program." By Nancy S. Theiss. *Oldham Era*, March 25, 2010, B1.

Morris, Louise. "The Living Treasures Program." By Nancy S. Theiss. *Oldham Era*, June 4, 2015, B1.

National Register of Historic Places. "Central LaGrange Historic District." 1988. U.S. Department of Interior, National Park Service, Washington, D.C.

New Era, April 23, 1903; May 17, 1903; August 9, 1903.

Oglesby, Nancy. "The Living Treasures Program." By Nancy S. Theiss. *Oldham Era*, April 12, 2012, B1.

Oldham Era. "1876–1926: 50 Years Anniversary." June 4, 1926.

———. "Historic Jerry's Corner Store to Be Auctioned Off Saturday." March 1, 1990, A6.

Oldson, Jimmie. "The Living Treasures Program." By Nancy S. Theiss. *Oldham Era*, November 8, 2012, A9.

Bibliography

Parker, W. Frank., ed. *Western Advertiser*, October 27, 1863.

Peak, Noah. "Memories of LaGrange Training School: A Tribute to the Legacy of Julius Rosenwald." *Courier-Journal* (Louisville, KY), August 8, 2013.

Peeples, William. "Buddy Pepper's Oldham County Line." *Courier-Journal & Times Magazine* (Louisville, KY), March 2, 1969, 15.

Prather, Charlie. "The Living Treasures Program." By Nancy S. Theiss. *Oldham Era*, December 13, 2007, B1.

Prisley, Sarah Jouette Taylor. *Taylor Family History*. Archival records, Monticello History Museum, Monticello, AR. N.d.

Rewell, George M. *Men of Mark*. Cleveland, OH: Geo. M. Ewell and Company, 1887.

Reynolds, Richard Coleman. "The Living Treasures Program." By Nancy S. Theiss. *Oldham Era*, May 27, 2021, A8.

Ricketts, Lucy Radcliffe. "The Living Treasures Program." By Nancy S. Theiss. *Oldham Era*, February 24, 2022, A8.

Riley, Barbara Hoffman. "The Living Treasures Program." By Nancy S. Theiss. *Oldham Era*, July 14, 2011, B1

Roberts, Jim. "The Living Treasures Program." By Nancy S. Theiss. *Oldham Era*, June 18, 2015, B1.

Simpson, Rev. R.N. "The Centennial of the LaGrange Christian Church 1845–1945." LaGrange, KY. 1945.

Smith, Dot. "The Living Treasures Program." By Nancy S. Theiss. *Oldham Era*, March 19, 2015, B1.

Spotts, Grace Parrott. "History of the First Baptist Church." LaGrange, KY. October 1, 1947.

Summitt, Dennis. "The Living Treasures Program." By Nancy S. Theiss. *Oldham Era*, July 24, 2019, B3.

Taylor, Reuben Thorton "Bookie." "Remembrances of Things Past." *The Era*, Centennial Celebration of LaGrange, October 1927.

Theiss, Nancy S. "History Infuses Meaning into Plaques' Designations." *Courier-Journal*, May 27, 2015, 6A.

———. *Oldham County: Life at the River's Edge*. Charleston, SC: The History Press, 2010.

Timmons, Nancy. "The Living Treasures Program." By Nancy S. Theiss. *Oldham Era*, February 19, 2015, B1.

Tingle, Mabel. "The Living Treasures Program." By Nancy S. Theiss. *Oldham Era*, July 23, 2009, B1.

Trabue, Alice Elizabeth. "Spring Hill, Oldham County, Ky. The Home of Major William Berry Taylor." *Register of the Kentucky State Historical Society*, May 1920.

Walters, Frances. "The Living Treasures Program." By Nancy S. Theiss. *Oldham Era*, August 18, 2016, B1.

White, Hazel Henson. "The Living Treasures Program." By Nancy S. Theiss. *Oldham Era*, April 18, 2019, B2.

About the Author

Nancy is a native of Oldham County, where she grew up on the family farm and married her childhood sweetheart. She has numerous degrees in education, biology and environmental studies. For her PhD, she studied ecologist and natural history author Aldo Leopold, who developed the first course—Wildlife Ecology 118 at the University of Wisconsin—to help teach people how to "read" the places where they live. She has taught in the public school system and worked for the Kentucky Department of Education and the Kentucky Department of Fish and Wildlife. She has been director of several nonprofits and currently works as the executive director of the Oldham County Historical Society. She has written history columns for the *Louisville Courier-Journal* and the *Oldham Era*, along with other articles and books, and has received numerous recognitions for her various endeavors. An avid naturalist and historian, Nancy believes that knowing your community and the people, places and living things (past and present) around you gives you an understanding of your importance and place in the world.